The
Christmas Plains

The
Christmas Plains

JOSEPH BOTTUM

IMAGE

NEW YORK

Published in the United States by Image,
an imprint of the Crown Publishing Group,
a division of Random House, Inc., New York.

WWW.CROWNPUBLISHING.COM

IMAGE is a registered trademark, and the "I" colophon is a
trademark of Random House, Inc.

Library of Congress Cataloging-in-Publication Data is
available upon request.

 ISBN 978-0-7704-3765-7
eISBN 978-0-7704-3766-4

Printed in the United States of America

Jacket design by Laura Duffy
Jacket photography © Kendra Perry-Koski

10 9 8 7 6 5 4 3 2 1

First Edition

In memory of my father

Contents

T HIS BOOK STARTED out as a small collection of essays about the meaning of Christmas. You know the sort of thing: a kind of "Yes,
Virginia, There Is a Santa Claus," that marvelous
piece of 1897 newspaper sentimentality, jazzed up
for modern audiences.

Unfortunately, I let down my guard, early on,
and my family and friends began crowding in. Old,
half-remembered Christmas decorations started
shouting for a place, and even those scratched red
saucer sleds my sisters and I had when we were
young clamored for a mention. Holiday dinners,
travelogues, the lyrics of carols, all the Christmas
books I've ever read—*everybody* wanted in on the

party. I sat down to write about how language works, and my daughter promptly marched in and refused to leave. Charles Dickens, that titan of the season, muscled his way into chapter after chapter. Even a small passage about the purpose of Advent nearly got itself trampled by recollections of childhood visits to my grandmother's. I tried to fight them off, but it wasn't much use. The intruders took over the house for their yuletide squabbles and celebrations, pretty much relegating me to the kitchen with orders to keep the food and drink coming and otherwise stay out of their way.

The result was supposed to be a set of five Christmas thoughts, interspersed with a handful of illustrative Christmas memories. Instead, it became a parade of reminiscences, broken only by the few moments when I was able to shout loudly enough above the holiday din to be heard on the meaning of it all. I'd apologize, but it's not really my fault. I blame the stubbornness of memories, the intemperate collection of people I've known in my life, and the sheer insanity that belongs to the Christmas season.

I should probably also mention that the stories wandering through this book are entirely true, if a little fictitious: the names changed, the timing telescoped, complicating detail ruthlessly expurgated, characteristics blithely shifted around, but otherwise pretty much how I remember things. Along the way, however, I made the mistake of consulting my aunts and uncles and cousins—consulting my wife and daughter, for that matter—and was sternly informed by any number of them that I had misremembered, gotten things wrong, taken liberties, ignored facts, and otherwise so mangled the truth that unless I carefully specified that everything I have to say is completely inaccurate, they would disown me.

The idea was tempting: losing all my familial complications in one swell foop. If nothing else, it would cut down on the telephone bills. But I love my family—as the years have gone by, I've even grown to like them—and I'd hate to lose them now. So let me simply note that, in memories as in automobiles, your mileage may vary.

The origins of mistletoe, the Christmas trees we had when I was young, the reason for the richness of yuletide food: to write about these topics has proved a strangely joyful activity, whether the thoughts and memories were bright or dark. But then, as Charles Dickens himself once observed, contemplation of Christmas is "never out of season." And since Dickens dominates the writing of the holiday, it's probably appropriate to let him have the last word, here in the winter cold: "God bless us, every one!"

—*The Black Hills*
December 2012

Chapter 1

See Amid the Winter

===============================

"I tell you what, my dear," said my aunt, one morning in the Christmas season when I left school: "as
this knotty point is still unsettled, and as we must
not make a mistake in our decision if we can help it,
I think we had better take a little breathing-time. In
the meanwhile, you must try to look at it from a new
point of view, and not as a schoolboy."

—*DAVID COPPERFIELD*

I

IT WAS IN the meadows along the little lake at
Cottonwood Springs, a hundred yards or so up
from the dam, that I saw the fox, red-brown against
the December snow. For decades after the Black
Hills were named a "national forest reserve" in 1897,

the government would exchange small pieces of land with ranchers along the edges, trading pastures for tree-grown lots. The result was a more natural, serrated line of dark spruce and ponderosa pine on the forest's border, but the reduction of open spaces within the protected woods—the loss of meadows like the one where I saw the fox this winter—also limited some of the land's support for small wildlife and the animals that hunt them.

Not that those western territories ever held a large population of predators. Cutting through the middle of the Dakotas, the Missouri River marks the boundary of the ancient glaciers that scraped out, to the east, a gentler countryside of softened plains and easy lakes. West of the river lies a different world, one that the Pleistocene ice never cleared. The Badlands and Black Hills, Bear Butte and Devils Tower—a rough landscape of broken prairie and high plateau that stretches five hundred miles from the Missouri to the Tetons.

And that country is just too thin, the winters

too hard, to feed many hunters. A single horned owl, fluffing its feathers on a gnarled cottonwood branch, will easily dominate two hundred acres of night hunting ground. A nesting pair of red-tail hawks will control a daylight range for an entire season. Add the superior small-game hunting of the coyotes, the depredations of the occasional mink or weasel down near the creek beds, the scavenging of the omnivore skunks and raccoons, and how much life is left in a lean land, especially over the winter?

Still, there was the fox, in a South Dakota meadow this past December, clear eyed and healthy, his dark brush lightly marking his back-trail in the snow. If you've ever seen mountain lions, you know how they pace: arrogant and powerful, as though they had greased machines coiling and uncoiling just beneath their skin. Coyotes slink through the yellow grass of the prairies, rough haired, scrawny, and cautious. Raccoons scurry, skunks blunder, and minks—well, it's hard to describe the behavior of minks. They seem to live a kind of vicious insanity, oddly matched with their rich fur and sweet faces. Foxes, however, are the strolling kind. Flashing white at their throats, with those black stockings around their paws, they pad through the fields like dandies ambling along the Paris pavement: inquisitive yet self-possessed, eager yet sensible, bold yet judicious.

We'd gone out to the area around the lake, my wife, Lorena, and I, with our daughter, Faith, to cut our annual Christmas tree. Lorena had stopped by the Forest Service office to pick up a harvesting permit days before, but we hadn't organized ourselves enough to accomplish our original plan of heading deep into the woods, back behind Crazy Horse or up toward Mount Rushmore. So we drove instead just a few miles west to look at a nearer place: tape measure, bow saw, and rope in hand, with Faith tugging along an old Flexible Flyer sled, its once red-painted runners tracing out their parallels in the snow behind her.

Every Christmas, during the years we lived

back east, I would hunt and hunt for the perfect tree. Maybe it had something to do with the feverish life we were living at the time, straining for some unknown perfection that always seemed just around the next bend. I had left the western world of my childhood intending only to go to college, but I stayed on the East Coast a little longer to finish graduate school. And then to teach, while I tried to find my footing as a writer. And then to complete some of that writing. And then to work on other people's writing as a magazine editor. And then . . .

About a decade ago, Lorena and I began to worry that we were letting too much of our time slip away—living homeless, in a peculiar kind of way: chasing from East Coast city to East Coast city, one new job after another, and providing for our daughter no clear geography in which she could center herself as she grew. Giving her no sense of place like the one I was given as a child, for good and for ill, out on those western plains. We needed a *foothold,* we decided, and what we found, at last, was a sprawling old Victorian monstrosity going cheap in the town of Hot Springs, down in the southern Black Hills.

We intended the house mostly as a playground, I think—a summer retreat that would serve the secondary purpose of allowing us to teach Faith western things: how to ride a horse, how to study the wildlife, how to climb the crumbling granite rocks. How to cut a tree, for that matter. But the ridiculous Black Hills house proved a help when, last fall, the eastern world in which I was working felt as though it was blowing up all around me. Lorena and I decided, in a sudden rush, that we needed to escape the craziness for a while. We said good-bye to our friends in Washington, DC, sublet our tiny apartment in New York City, and fled out, for the winter, to that summer place in the hills—hoping, I think, just to get a little breathing room. A little distance from which to think about it all.

Anyway, back in our East Coast days, I would drive like a man possessed through the slush-filled

streets of Washington at Christmastime—up
Georgia Avenue to Silver Spring or down through
Georgetown and over the bridge to Arlington—
going from lot to lot in anxious search of the ideal
height, the best spread, the proper fullness of the
branches. While I was working in New York, I
would spend a fortune on taxis down to Greenwich
Village, up to Central Park, across town to those
seasonal tree stands along the West Side Highway.
But at some point—maybe around the time we left
New York for South Dakota—I seem to have given
up on perfection in Christmas trees.

Given up on perfection in other things, too, it
may be. Still, we had been spoiled by the model
cones of thick evergreens for sale in the cities back
east. The dry western lands grow a thinner tree
with sparser branches, and a good Christmas tree
from the Black Hills typically has character rather
than flawlessness: an eccentric limb trained up at
angle, an interesting twist in the trunk. And that's
what we were hunting for—Lorena, Faith, and

I—as we hiked up the hill to cut this year's tree, our breath rough in the afternoon sun.

It proved a surprisingly hard climb. Under the dusting of the morning snow, yesterday's crust would hold each footstep just long enough to hint that it would support us before we broke through, ankle deep. Knee deep in the drifts. I stopped for a moment to rest, and it was then, looking back down toward the lake, that I saw the fox, pausing as he padded on the snow's surface across the meadow.

His clever sharp face, those alert pointed ears. I don't know how exactly to explain it, but he seemed somehow wildly alive at that instant: a curious, observant creature, both fascinated by and satisfied with the world that God and nature had set around him. He studied the lake shrewdly, as though considering whether the cottontails would come down to the shore to drink. He glanced up at the leeward woods, where his rank scent had made the chipmunks and red squirrels chitter angrily in the trees. He cocked his head, listening for the rustle of winter mice in the grass beneath the snow. Dozens of possibilities seemed to lie before him—all interesting, all worth pursuing in their proper time.

Then Faith called out to say she'd found the tree, the exact tree she'd been searching for, just over the hill. And by the time we measured it, and walked around it, arguing its points, and sawed through its trunk, and bound it to the sled, and pulled it back up over the hill, the fox had made his choice and was gone. We packed up, tied the tree to the roof of the car, and drove carefully up the snow-packed road, heading home to begin setting up for Christmas. My first Christmas back in South Dakota since I was a child.

II

I GUESS I should have known, or reasonably expected, that a return to places I knew in childhood would trigger memories: every step kicking up the past, like the dust that trails up behind us on a dirt road. But what I hadn't quite counted on was the magnifying effect of Christmas, for something in the design of the holiday seems determined to bring our childhoods back upon us. An exaggerated past, too, even if we mean to be strictly honest: After my father died, I found among his things an old cartoon he had clipped from somewhere. *The New Yorker,* maybe, or some other magazine. It showed a man and a boy standing in their front doorway after a winter storm. "This is nothing," says the man, waist-high in snow. "When I was your age, the snow came to *here,*" raising his hand to his chin. And there's the boy, wide-eyed, with the snow all the way up to his chin.

Lorena and I had run off to South Dakota to think of a way forward, a new choice for our lives. But then Christmas came upon us, and with it, the rush of memory that will not be denied: rich, thick, and often deeply annoying. My daughter hunches down in dread as we drive through the winter hills these days, knowing that every passing rock and side road is likely to provoke some tale of her father's childhood, some entry in the mythology of his western self.

And yet, even as I tell her the old Christmas stories, I notice what may be the most curious feature of memory—for the stories themselves are not what we have to struggle to remember. Stirred up by a visit home, aggravated by the power of Christmas, occasions for remembering hurl themselves at us like ice storms, whether we want them or not. No, it's not the facts but the *feelings,* the sharp emotions we felt at the time, that fail us, slipping into indistinction even while we tell our stories of the past.

I can call up moment after moment of precise memory from the Christmases of my childhood, like frozen frames of recollection: A sparrow, its feathers so fluffed for warmth it looked like a fat monk in a robe and tonsure, peering out from the ice-wrapped lilac hedge while I sat at the living room window, waiting for my parents to wake.

The sideways tilt of my father's head as he looked down in concentration, cutting out the sections of a grapefruit for Christmas breakfast. The heft of the new Swiss Army knife from my uncle, smuggled in the pocket of my dress pants to church. The steam rising while we washed the endless piles of dishes after Christmas dinner, until the fog condensed in rivulets that raced each other down the kitchen windowpanes to pool on the painted sill.

I can call up nearly everything—except the sensation, the overwhelming waves that beat upon my sisters and me down the long stream of days in the Christmas season when we were young. To think again about those times is more to recall that we had a certain feeling than it is to recapture just how that feeling actually felt. The memories come faded, like last year's pine needles: the few that always seem to find their way in among the Christmas ornaments, to sift out yellow and brittle when the box comes down from the back of the linen closet the next December.

Why should I remember the heavy-scented balsam tree we had when I was six? The long-needled ponderosa, drooping under the weight of its ornaments, when I was eight? The Douglas fir, the juniper? The scallop-leaved holly set out on the sideboard and mantel with a stern warning every year not to eat the berries? The silly-looking plastic mistletoe my mother would hang, giggling with my father over a joke they wouldn't explain?

There in Pierre, South Dakota, when I was young—and later, when my parents had moved us out to Utah—I was happy, I suppose, and I was sad, but *happy* and *sad* are always lies, of a sort: the words we use to smooth the sharp edges off our memories and sand them down to generalities. Think of the parallel with *hot* and *cold*: I realize now, in retrospect, that the houses of my childhood were simultaneously too warm and too cool. The clanking furnaces kept them overheated from September to April, a dry heat that dulled out within a year the gloss in the painted window frames and cracked down the middle the door of the china cupboard. But those western houses were drafty as well. All winter the wind screamed down the frozen plains from Canada, clawing through the weather stripping and the storm windows and the door seals and the crumbling mortar of the cinderblock foundations.

And yet, I don't remember actually being any general thing like hot or cold. What I remember is lying on the living room floor alongside the burbling radiator, propped up on my elbows and a cushion filched from the sofa, to read Gerald Durrell's *My Family and Other Animals* while the sweat dripped inside my shirt and the wind whistled up through the gap around the radiator pipe to chill my hands. So, too, I don't remember being happy or sad. There were happy things and sad things, moments of strange fear and moments of lopsided comedy, tumbled together in such complete immediacy I had neither space nor time to rise above them and call them by some generic name.

Our days move differently now, of course. A few weeks ago, Lorena reminded me we had only a month in which to clear away enough work to take a trip we had scheduled—and then she began to laugh, asking, "Do you remember when a month seemed a *long* time?" It might stand as the surest marker of the difference between childhood and age: a month was once forever, and now it's just a month. Or less.

One Saturday, back when she was a toddler, Faith spent the morning talking about the planned visit that afternoon of her friend Rose, the child of a South Dakotan friend settled back east in Washington. On and on she prattled happily—until, finally, she sat down on the stairs to sob in . . . what? Frustration? Exhaustion? Yearning? It does no good to say that she was overexcited, the way parents do, the way Lorena and I did. That's experience seen from the outside, emotion risen above and understood. We could hold the little girl and comfort her and wait for it to pass. But the essence of what she was feeling: all that is gone from us now. Now that we are older.

III

WELL, MAYBE NOT *completely* gone. I remember, for instance, that I was filled with something I now understand as fury, that winter before Christmas the year I was fourteen. The reason still isn't clear. It was fury at my parents, fury at my sisters, fury when I was treated like a child, fury when I was treated like an adult, fury at the sheer *being* of being fourteen years old. The inwardness of the feeling seems impossible to call up again—primarily, I think, because even then it had no real content. It was a kind of pure hunger, an unsatisfiable, unending ache without focus, object, or goal. I wanted to be noticed all the time, and I wanted to be invisible, passing through the world unseen. I wanted to be cared for, and I wanted to be unencumbered with care. I wanted everything. I wanted nothing. I just wanted.

A portion of it may have been actual hunger. For mothers, when their sons' growth kicks in, it must seem as though something unimaginably alien has moved into the house. I remember needing food all the time. As I walked in the door after school, I would tear open a plastic-wrapped tube of Fig Newtons. Before supper, I would eat wax-paper package after wax-paper package of graham crackers—buttering them, it now seems hard to believe, to make them more filling—and still down two or three helpings of the roast my mother put on the table two hours later.

There was an extravagance to eating and drinking at that age which cannot be recreated at any other point in life. I remember the rain splashing against the windows while I sat at the speckled linoleum of the kitchen table on a Saturday afternoon with a loaf of sandwich bread, a bag of apples, and a jar of peanut butter, filling the pages of *The Count of Monte Cristo* with apple crumbs and peanut-buttered thumbprints. I remember swallowing gulp after gulp of water from the silver arc of the garden hose after mowing the lawn in the heat of a summer evening—and then, my belly so distended I could barely move, falling back on the new-cut grass to watch the angry gnats swirl up against the orange sunset.

But the feeling of being fourteen was something more than just appetite. All that winter before Christmas, the lintels of the doors through the house were marked with handprints as I reached up to touch them every time I passed beneath, amazed at my new height. I had spent my fall weekends hauling hay—the worst job I've ever had—and I was proud of my new strength. We'd often visit our grandparents over in Rapid City, staying in the Black Hills during the summers, but my parents had been defined by the hard Dakota prairie, I think, back in my hometown of Pierre, and they believed in work for their children. By the time I left home for good, I'd delivered papers early in the morning, and scooped ice cream after school, and followed a harvest team through the wheat fields, and spent a month with a finish-carpentry crew, tacking the wooden trim on kitchens through an endless subdivision of identical split-level houses in Ogden, Utah.

Whenever one job ended, there was some new client of my father's law practice, anxious—my father always insisted—for me to come along and help. I stood behind the taco grill, hour after hour, waiting for customers at a failing Mexican fast-food restaurant, and I hung pictures at an art gallery, briefly and badly. At a placer-wash California gold mine outside Nevada City, the summer I was fifteen, I learned how to run a diesel pumping engine and mix the orange and purple glues that held together the huge sections of plastic pipe that carried water up to the mine. I learned to play pinochle at night by kerosene lantern and to sit all afternoon, watching for leaks in the 150-foot wooden sluice we'd built, lined with crosshatched steel frames on hairy mats to catch the washed-down gold that, sadly, wasn't there.

For my parents, the point wasn't the money—which was good, because I managed to save none of it. I never did get paid for the summer at the gold mine. The leasing firms came in August to repossess the bulldozer and the backhoe, the sheriffs followed the next day with an eviction notice, and the mining company that was going to make us all rich dissolved in the usual muddle of liens and bankruptcies, lawsuits and countersuits, that seemed to await the would-be wheeler-dealers and Micawberish romantics of business who passed through our lives. You have to imagine men with a brilliant, daring idea for making a third fortune by buying up time-share leases with the money from their second fortune, which they would make by speculating on wheat futures with the money from their first fortune, which they would make by running a mail-order business—which they were planning to start any day now, as soon as they could raise the money. These people were their own pyramid scheme.

Even the cash from the jobs for which I actually got paid seemed to disappear beyond any accounting. Some of it got used to buy books—and more books, a few phonograph albums, and yet more books. Why would anyone use the Carnegie Library down by the courthouse when it was possible to *own* a book: hold it, feel the possession of it while you were reading, then set it as a permanent marker on the shelves beside all the other books? More of it went in Christmas presents, the extravagance of the season, and the rest seemed simply to get lost, frittered away in living.

Once, while I was back from college over Christmas break, my father sent me off for a week to Portland with an enormous, laughing, wild-living man from Denver named Edward Reynard: a former football player, a promoter of impossible schemes, a teller of stories, a buyer of drinks, a thief if the occasion offered, and the best-dressed man I have ever known. We were supposed to close down a failing space heater company before the vultures picked it apart: get an inventory, cancel the outstanding orders, change the locks, and pack up the hopelessly confused paperwork for the accountants to look at. I'm not sure, even now, quite how an eighteen-year-old philosophy student was going to protect anyone's interests. The idea may simply have been that Edward Reynard was there to see that the company's officers didn't loot the place down to the carpets, and I was there to see that he didn't join in.

But mostly what I remember is the style of the man I traveled with. He acted as though the most important reason for the trip was the opportunity to taste again a kind of pickle made only in Portland, and he carried me from bar to bar, insisting that I'd be grateful the rest of my life for understanding the distinctions among piano bars and hotel bars and nightclubs and the kind of neighborhood bars where they put thick peppermint candy canes as swizzle sticks in hot Christmas drinks.

The first morning we were there, he walked in to find me trying to figure out how to use the coffee-maker that slid out of a cupboard in the hotel room. Stopping me—and insisting I put on a jacket and tie—he took me downstairs to the linen-covered tables, sprigs of Christmas holly in little silver vases. And it was there, once the china cups and coffee had come, that he explained the code of men like himself. Gentlemen, he said (and it was the first time I had ever heard the word used in any but a mocking way), gentlemen—ladies, for that matter, all people who want to live well—never cook for themselves. When they have money, they eat in restaurants. When they are broke, they go hungry. It was his great boast that, whatever else he had done in his life to survive, he had never tried to economize even to the extent of boiling water for himself.

I liked cooking too much to agree, but the *stance* of it—the Renaissance-courtier quality of the scruple, the antiquated arrogance, the marking of a point of honor, the proud claiming of an absolute adherence to a style of living—seemed at the time an ideal of adulthood.

IV

THAT WAS PROBABLY not the lesson my parents had in mind when they sent their children off to work. My sisters were perpetually tardy night owls, barely convinced the sun rises before noon, and, compared with me, they were both bright-eyed and bushy-tailed. Except perhaps for the presents waiting under the tree on Christmas Day, I can't remember anything that could make us get up in the morning when we didn't have to. Faced with children like this, our mother and father no doubt hoped work would teach us early rising—and steadiness and thrift and application and all the rest of the conscientious virtues that remained common coin on the western plains long after the rest of America became too self-conscious to hold them openly. "When you wake up, get up; when you get up, do something," my father would intone in the carefully righteous voice of a man handing on to his children the ancient wisdom of his forebears.

In fact, we were bombarded with lots of such things while I was growing up—daily doses of the kind of adage with which Benjamin Franklin peppered *Poor Richard's Almanack* back in the eighteenth century: "A penny saved is a penny earned," "Plow deep while sluggards sleep," "Never leave till tomorrow what you can do today." But they had lost, somehow, their content and purpose, and you can trace, in that loss, the history of a certain swath of America. My great-grandparents, all eight of them original settlers in South Dakota, actually lived their lives by Franklin's maxims. Their children, my grandparents, merely believed them. And by the time those stern aphorisms reached my parents' generation, they had become something not far removed from knocking on wood to avert the evil eye or curving out to keep from walking under a ladder: the things people do or say with that apologetic shrug which means they know they shouldn't still half-believe such superstitious old-fashionedness.

The long decades of attack on the virtues of the middle class had taken their toll. Even in Pierre, about as far from the centers of avant-garde culture as one can reasonably get, it made the people we knew uneasy and awkward in their skins—and they could not plead success as the justification for their lives, for South Dakota had seen too much failure. Those hard prairies and badlands were the graveyard of the immigrants' dream. The state reached its peak of population not in recent years but all the way back in the 1880s, when homesteading called in over a million settlers in what was called the "Dakota Boom."

Twenty-five years later—after the blizzards, the droughts, the floods, and the locust plagues, after the summers of broiling heat and winters of endless cold—there were scant thousands of them left. The banks and the feed stores in the county seats were boarded up. The farmers abandoned their hopeless plowing. The ranchers gave up when they saw their cattle freezing at Christmas and dying of thirst on the Fourth of July. The deserted wooden churches lasted for a few more years, turning gray in the relentless wind, before they fell in upon themselves.

The settlers who survived were luckier and better placed, nearer the rivers but off the floodplains, closer to the markets at the railheads, sheltered by the hills from some of the worst of the winters. They were harder, too: stern, unyielding people who did not fail, because they refused to. But their descendants grew less stern and more yielding, generation by generation—a weaker, more diffident people, uncertain of the virtues they ought to pursue and unsure of how to pursue them.

V

AND YET, IT would be wrong to say that my own parents had lost—at least for their children—their entire share in the old-fashioned American vision of the complete citizen. What they still held, deeply and truly, was the other side of the Ben Franklin ideal: the eighteenth-century model of a world in which Franklin could be a printer and an inventor and a statesman and a writer and a builder and a scientist and a diplomat. My father and mother still believed in an old-fashioned *omnicompetence*: the capacity for everything, the ability to turn one's hand to anything.

Not, you understand, that they ever managed for themselves the omnicompetence they preached, or that we children ever lived up to their expectations. But the ideal ruled our childhoods, and it was the most impractical practicality anyone ever conceived. I have a photograph of the three of us posed against the railing of the ferry crossing Lake

Michigan on our way to Boston for a family vacation one year. I suppose I must have been eleven, which would have made my older sister twelve and my younger sister perhaps six. And that knock-kneed boy and those rail-thin girls were supposed to be able to trim a Christmas tree and ride a horse, cook a dinner and use a drill, pick out a melody on the piano and clean the points on the station wagon's distributor.

Exactly why did my father want us to understand how to rewire the toaster? Or at least, since that's not necessarily a bad thing to know, why did he insist we be able to rewire the toaster *and* recite all 108 lines of Edgar Allan Poe's "The Raven"? *Ah, distinctly I remember it was in the bleak December* (First make sure the toaster is unplugged) *and each separate dying ember* (Now take a Phillip's-head screwdriver) *wrought its ghost upon the floor* (I said a Phillip's-head. A Phillip's-head. The one with the pointy cross on the end). *Eagerly I wished the morrow* (Finally. Now turn the toaster over and look for the screws on the bottom), *vainly I had sought to borrow* (Um, yes, I did forget about the crumbs falling out all over the kitchen floor) *from my books surcease of sorrow* (No, your mother is not going to be mad), *sorrow for the lost Lenore* (Yes, I'm sure). *For the rare and radiant maiden whom the angels name Lenore* (That's all right. It's supposed to spring out like that), *nameless here for evermore* (See? That's where the insulation has worn through). *And the silken sad uncertain rustling of each purple curtain* (Yes, that's why the fuse blew this morning. No, you can't plug it back in and watch it spark) *thrilled me—filled me with fantastic terrors never felt before.*

The poor workers who passed through the house to repair things—or re-repair the things we had mangled trying to fix them ourselves—were turned into adjunct professors at my parents' Academy for Teaching Children Everything. I don't know why, it may have been the wide-eyed look of innocence my mother reserved for strangers from whom she wanted something, but most of them were charmed by the demand that they explain each step of their work to three skinny and skeptical children. I remember sitting with my little sister fully clothed in the dry bathtub, resting our chins on the porcelain edge, while a tongue-tied plumber, sweating in nervousness, tried simultaneously to wrestle a new toilet into place and to explain what the wax ring at the joint was for. The dry cleaner, the milkman, and the driver of the cement mixer were expected to have the history of their professions at their fingertips. The Culligan Man, wheeling in his water-softening tank, gave us a surprisingly good explanation of pH levels and the buffering of salt solutions. (You see? I remember it to this day.) Even the lady collecting for UNICEF had to deliver a potted lecture on the goals of the United Nations before we were allowed to drop our pennies in her orange box.

Meanwhile, we had *Learning About the Great Composers* phonograph records and *Build Your Own Shortwave Radio* kits and Chilton car-repair manuals and booklets called *Teach Yourself the*

Guitar in 12 Easy Lessons. We had reel-to-reel tapes of Allen Ginsberg reciting his poetry, and Vincent Price overacting his way through Shakespeare's soliloquies, and Senator Dirksen declaiming the Gettysburg Address and other great speeches of American history.

The year I was ten, my mother decided she would finish her graduate degree in dramatics, and it never occurred to her not to take her children with her for a summer at the Black Hills Playhouse, over in the western part of the state— for what better chance could there be for us to see how to put on a play? We learned stage carpentry from the set-builders and silk screening from the promotion department. We danced and sneered as the wicked children in a production of *Carousel,* and we annoyed the workshop actors all summer by reciting along with them their lines in rehearsals for Jean-Paul Sartre's *No Exit.* "Hell is other people," my little sister would snarl when we tried to get her up in the morning. She was better at the line—more existentially despairing—than the actual cast.

A childhood like this was fun, of course, and aggravating beyond belief. One August, while I was in college at Georgetown, a friend from home came east to visit. I remember, for that was the summer I caught pneumonia while setting up cocktail parties for a catering company in the evenings, working on a cleanup crew for a construction company in the mornings, and sleeping through my philosophy classes in the afternoons. And as we sat on the brick steps of a rented student house on Observatory Place, talking and drinking gin while the humid Washington evening sweated around us, she told me that she had decided not to go on to graduate school in literature but to enroll in law school, because, she joked, the only thing she wanted in life was to be rich—not *rich* rich, necessarily, but rich enough that she could hire people to do things for her and never have to bother with learning how to do them herself.

We laughed and laughed, so hard I dropped my drink, and then we laughed at that, for we had reached the stage of both reminiscence and drinking where everything seems impossibly funny. But she had reminded me of the less pleasant side of my parents' desire for omnicompetent children. The truth is, learning to do a little bit of everything, we never learned to do anything well. The attempt to be all things is a recipe to be nothing. And there always loomed over us an unfulfillable demand that we would, somehow, already know how to do each new task—and when he was too tired or irritated to catch himself, the demand would smash out in frustration from my father.

I remember my little sister crying on her first skiing trip, ruining a Christmas outing up the canyons outside Salt Lake City, because she was afraid to tell him she didn't know how to ski. I remember his taking me trapshooting when I was eight—and stalking out to snatch his shotgun back in disgust when I missed six shots in a row. I remember his barking, "Why are you so *incompetent?*" when my older sister brought him the wrong hammer. It was the worst insult we could imagine, and she sobbed and sobbed alone in her room until my mother sent him in to apologize.

Those nervous, apprehensive moments were rare, but we would do anything to avoid them, and what we learned to do was to fake it: fake understanding blank verse, fake knowing how to rewire the strings of Christmas lights, fake being able to reassemble the clutch on the pickup. It was a kind of constant pretense of knowledge in the face of the unknown, and my mother and father intended it to be born from self-confidence. But to their disappointment, I was an anxious child, and its real root was a fear of being discovered not to know, a fear of being found out false.

It's only now, while I bring up my own daughter, that I realize how cleverly my parents had tried to escape the trap in which they found themselves. They were cultured people at a time in which their culture had turned against itself. They were old-fashioned South Dakotans trying—with the best will in the world, a real desire for accommodation—to remake themselves in a new-fashioned time.

And their solution was not to abandon the Ben Franklinism in which they had grown up, but to invert it: a model of middle-class virtues transformed into a model of a different sort. *Poor Richard's* "Never leave till tomorrow what you can do today" became "Never leave anything untried." The demand for hard work, which for Franklin was an adjunct of thrift, became for my parents a tool of experience. Their vision was intermittent, for I think they never brought the idea of a Franklinesque life to full consciousness. But they wanted something new for themselves and their children, and what they came up with was, in its way, brilliant and lively and filled with adventure.

VI

IT WAS ALSO doomed, as I learned when I went off to work and discovered that having had someone explain to me how an arc-welding machine works isn't the same as actually being able to weld. Once, when I was working for a construction company that was building a new wing on a pharmaceutical factory, the crew boss asked if I knew how to hang a door. I'd been working all summer, and I felt competent—as though confidence and a general ability to figure things out would carry me through most anything. Besides, I'd taken wooden doors off their hinges at home, planing them down to make them fit after they'd warped, and none of it seemed too hard.

But what he pointed me to wasn't like the finished jambs and sills at home. It was a raw hole in a half-finished wall. And there beside it on the floor was a massive metal frame and a steel door so heavy I could barely lift it, much less maneuver it onto its hinges or use it (as I originally planned) as a giant pattern with which to square the frame before I attached it to the wall. He let me work on that door for hours, never saying a word, until finally, by chance, I got the frame straight enough to fit and wiggled the door onto its hinges. That's when he walked over and said—more to the door than to me, swinging it gently back and forth—"Don't ever say you know how to do something when you don't."

I must have been sixteen that summer, and the shame of his soft rebuke seemed overwhelming. I took such things hard, because . . . oh, because I was sixteen and I was filled with a hunger to be something complete, to have the kind of natural authority that crew boss had: the weight of it, the gravity of a man who actually knows. I didn't really want to understand how to hang a door. I wanted to understand the secret of grown-ups. I wanted to be initiated in the gnostic mysticism of adulthood. I wanted the truth of it—and the people who awakened that desire were invariably cast as surrogate parents.

It's a wonder they didn't run away screaming. Who needs his job to entail the semi-adoption of half-grown children with aching holes in their psyches? Besides, I already had, with my own parents, as much parenting as I could use in one lifetime. But there's something deep in the architecture of children that seeks more of mothers and fathers than actual mothers and fathers can ever be.

That's why, I suppose, I spent long years doing little but hunting for extra parents. The boss at the gold mine was a talker named Sam Sheridan, a man who could tell a joke, shape almost anything that happened to him into a story, and charm investors into putting up the cash for any number of his half-baked schemes. But mostly what I remember is his constant patter, the commentary that poured out from him while we worked—always culminating in some claim of universal law, coined for the occasion. As we realigned the rollers on the twenty-foot perforated drum that spiraled out the rocks too big to wash down the sluice, he'd say, "The rule to remember is: When something's broken, first you bang on it a little, then you curse at it a little, and then you go and get a bigger hammer." As we reconnected the linkage for the vibrating table, he'd explain, "The lesson here is: Some baling wire, some duct tape, and there's nothing you can't patch up."

But then, too, out on the ranch, there was a rider who seemed almost never to speak at all. If I knew his name, I've forgotten it now, but I have a memory—like one of those gray-edged snapshots from the little Bakelite plastic cameras my grandparents gave us when I was eight—of sitting beside him on the bunkhouse steps one evening while he worked on a brittle piece of old leather and watched the enormous orange sun setting over the yellow hills. I remember his browned face and dusty clothes. I remember the dark sweat stain behind the brown plait that circled his hat. I remember, as a perpetual model of adulthood, his ability to sit silent and self-possessed for hours, calmly rubbing oil into the leather until the light failed. And I longed to learn how to be that man—and to be Sam Sheridan, and to be Edward Reynard, all rolled together, all at once.

Of course, even as children, my sisters and I had a pretty clear sense that we weren't actually going to succeed at being all things. I imagine that's one of the reasons I was so unbearable the winter I was fourteen. Already I saw the thinning down of things, the fading of possibility, and I was furious at what seemed the unfairness of it all. What I wanted was to be *everything*: a scholar and a cowboy, a poet and a politician, a wheeling-dealing stock promoter and a Trappist monk, singing the psalms with his brothers on Christmas morning. The combination didn't seem unreasonable at the time, but I felt, somehow, that my mother and father were thwarting my attempts to make it come true. Mark this thought, for it is the key to how adolescent boys view the world: The very people who were responsible for what I wanted, the ones who put that desire in me, wouldn't let me fulfill it. Why, it was so . . . unfair. That's what it was. Unfair.

VII

THERE WAS A story kicking around when I was young, about the Christmas some of my grandfather's friends delivered a baby. I'd heard parts of it, I think, here and there, but the first time I remember listening to it, all the way through, was after my grandfather died. I'd been driving across the country, one of those summers while I was in college, and I stopped in Rapid City to visit the family graves, the family friends. And over lunch, one of my grandfather's cronies, an insurance agent named Will Christiansen, told me the tale.

To this day, I'm not sure why. It may be that he thought I was growing too bookish and needed reminding of the impracticality of an academic life and the helplessness of intellectual types. Certainly that was the moral in the way he told the story, and if I took away a different lesson—well, that was hardly his fault. He'd done his duty, as he saw it, by his old friend's grandchild.

Anyway, the story, as I piece it together today in memory, has that kind of timeless quality that derives mostly from lacking detail. It was in the 1940s, or maybe the 1950s, or maybe even the early 1960s—who knows?—but once, years ago, just before Christmas, a judge from Minneapolis was bringing his brother out to western South Dakota. Now, the brother, as I understand it, was a college professor, an economist of some sort, and they gathered up another acquaintance of my grandfather's, a political lawyer from St. Paul, to come out and see the Badlands and the Black Hills dusted with snow. So they dropped down through Minnesota, over to Brookings, and then west across rural South Dakota. And it was there, somewhere in the rough country past the Missouri, that they saw the girl, flagging them down from the side of the road.

She was young and cold, and scared, I assume, and her mother needed help, she said, up on the farm, a mile or more off the highway. So they wrapped the child up in their overcoats, brought her inside the warm car, and turned onto the dirt track to the farmhouse. What they found was a pregnant woman late in heavy contractions. She'd planned to head into town after Christmas to wait for the baby, she told them between gasps, but the labor started hard and early, with the phone line down. Her husband was off in the army, she said, and her own mother had gone into town for the day.

So those highly trained, seriously educated men put on water to boil, because they didn't know what else to do. And guided by the woman—who had been through it before, after all—they sterilized the kitchen towels and helped deliver a baby, there on the linoleum floor. All that blood, the primal exposure, the mess, the emergence of the newborn boy, his first squalls: They felt, I imagine, unimportant and vital, all at the same time. Awed and earthy, all together. Powerless and brave. Afterward, they cleaned the mother as best they could and carried her and the newborn child up to bed. The professor mopped up, the lawyer sat with the mother and baby, and the judge, with the older girl to direct him, drove thirty miles into town to find some help.

Now, the funny part, as Mr. Christiansen told the story, happened once the judge found help, and the neighbor women came bustling in. Within minutes, the incompetent men from the city had been eased out—thanked profusely but pushed firmly out of the bedroom and, soon enough, out of the farmhouse and out of those country people's lives. In something of a huff, they loaded themselves back in their fancy car to finish the drive to Rapid City. But I imagine they felt changed, that Christmas with my grandparents in the Black Hills. How could they not? They had saved that woman, in the sense that she might have died without them, but they could also have killed her, and the baby, by not knowing what they were doing—by not being competent. Faced with real life, they proved fumblers and fools. And yet, those three men did what they could, when they had to, and they stayed. Which, as I listened to the story, makes them seem wise.

We experience so little that we can be certain is no abstraction—so little that comes to us unfiltered through social lenses, intellectual layers, or the filmy gauze of self-interest and self-absorption. Great pain and death, of course: the experience of holding a dying person. Prayer, sometimes: the disappearance of the self in the encounter with God. The shock of a lightning bolt, just outside the kitchen window. And childbirth: the unstoppable, undeniable appearance of new life.

Perhaps that has something to do with why I felt so uneasy, uncomfortable in my bones, early that winter I was fourteen. Oh, most of it was surely just the strangeness of being fourteen, but I could sense, even in the midst of those adolescent confusions, some widening distance from the root of life. Yes, a kind of loss is written into all human action, for our possibilities decline as we use them: every choice eliminates the other choices we didn't make; no chances stay forever. But this was something more than simply the logic of growing up. Even among those endless possibilities my parents had tried to form—to teach me, like that winter fox I saw this Christmas, to be perpetually pleased with the universe of choices all around—I could perceive few options that connected with the deep, raw stuff of God and life and death. To be a tourist in this world is to collect marvelous adventures and experiences, but it is also a way of never quite belonging.

Whatever I was feeling in those months before Christmas, it faded quickly enough, once the season itself began—my adolescent irritation and disengagement drowned by the rush of carols and Advent calendars and the hunt for presents. By the candles and decorations and the balsam fir my parents brought home from the Boy Scouts' Christmas tree stand in the church parking lot. By the wreaths and mistletoe and the annual agony of untangling the Christmas lights. By the sheer gale of the holiday, blowing across the prairie like a winter storm.

And that's as it should be, yes? We could speak here of Christmas as a symbol of unity and connection: rejoining with the family, reestablishing a spiritual understanding of the world. And it would be true enough. We feel that sense of belonging and association when we let Christmas wash over us, when we allow it to sweep us up in its tide. Christmas genuinely works as a symbol because, during the holiday's season, we make an extra effort to spend time with our families and wish goodwill to the people we meet. To drop a few coins in the red Salvation Army kettle down at the mall, for that matter, while the man in the Santa Claus suit rings his silver bell.

We do those things, however, because Christmas is not a symbol. Not really. Not down at the root. The symbolic value of the holiday derives from a reality beyond all abstractions: A child delivered in the straw of a stable. A figure born to teach us faith and hope and charity. A savior come to ransom us from death. The son of God descended in the flesh.

The deep stuff, in other words: the meaning at which all our sense of Christmas aims.

Chapter 2

Angels We Have Heard

Seasonable tokens are about. Red berries shine here
and there in the lattices of Minor Canon Corner;
Mr. and Mrs. Tope are daintily sticking sprigs of
holly into the carvings and sconces of the Cathedral
stalls, as if they were sticking them into the coat-
button-holes of the Dean and Chapter. Lavish pro-
fusion is in the shops. . . . In short, Cloisterham is up
and doing.

—*THE MYSTERY OF EDWIN DROOD*

I

WHEN I WAS young—no, even today: All my
life, Christmas has begun with the words.
Bethlehem and *sleigh bells, crèches* and *chestnuts,*

Wise Men and *mangers,* that storm of Christmas language that sweeps down upon us every December. It's like the mad glitter of winter sun through the ice that wraps the spruce and pine. It's like the drift of snowflakes through the yellow circle of a street light, late at night. It's like the angels dancing.

Reindeer and *swaddling clothes, Santa* and *tinsel, poinsettias* and *shepherds, candy canes* and *sore afraid,* all those words and phrases we use almost only at Christmas. They rise and fall, join and part, then turn and join again. Forget, for a moment, what they mean, the things they try to name, and just watch them as they weave through their riotous Christmas waltzes: hundreds of them in frenzied caracoles and strange cotillions. Their swirl has the feeling of a pattern, although it's too complex to grasp completely, like the intricate symmetry of snowflakes, just below the reach of sight, or the fractals of December frost, traced with a finger on a bedroom window. I could sense it often, I think, when I was a child. Sometimes I see it still, dancing just beyond comprehension. *There,* on the edge of prayer. *There,* on the edge of sleep.

And it came to pass . . . no room for them in the inn . . . keeping watch . . . fear not . . . tidings of great joy. Sometimes language speaks to us in odd ways—as though there were a great enchantment in this world, a sudden gift of meaning, a light that plays on the objects and actions scattered around our lives. And we all knew it, as children. The magic can fade, of course, as we grow older: fade so much that even Christmas has trouble bringing it back. Still, the experience itself, the way words sparkled as we used them—that was real, when we were young.

One morning near Christmas—back while we lived in Washington: that brick place on Park Road, with the traffic roaring by—my daughter, Faith, four years old at the time, marched into the kitchen to announce, "*Thwart* is a good word." And then she marched out again. She was a proclaimer in those days: a pronouncer, a declarer of what she had just discerned as steadfast, unalterable truths. A day or two earlier that same Christmas season, she padded into my room, thoughtful in her footsie pajamas, and attempted an experiment. We'd picked up at a neighbor's yard sale one of those tall old filing cabinets—really old: army surplus in chipped olive green—with five drawers that slid out in long rows. For some reason, Faith liked to climb up and sit on it, an elevated throne from which to survey the room while she made pronouncements to her stuffed animals. And usually she reached her perch by dragging over a chair, crawling from the chair to a table top, and scrambling up to join her animals from there.

This time, however, she thought she'd try something different. While I worked, attempting in my slow way to write at my desk, she slipped past and carefully pulled out the bottom drawer, opening it all the way. Then she slid out the fourth drawer most of the way, and the third drawer a little less, and the second a little less than that . . . until she had constructed for herself a file-filled stairway. Which she mounted, only to find that her even her slight weight unbalanced the wobbly thing. The filing cabinet leaned toward her just enough to make the other drawers come sliding out.

Fortunately, the fully extended bottom drawer caught on the floor, holding the weight of the cabinet and keeping it from tumbling down on top of her. But the higher drawers, rolling open, slapped into her and threw her back to land with a gasp and a thump on the floor. I spun around just in time to see the cabinet totter once or twice, as though it were thinking—in its calm, deliberate way—about how to swivel away from the support of the bottom drawer and smash to pieces. In the end, almost regretfully, it settled for falling back into place with a crash that shook the house. And from her seat on the floor, Faith looked up at me in the loud silence to announce—in the tone of someone conveying an absolute truth to a slightly dim audience—"That was not a good idea."

I doubt I've been as confident about anything, in adulthood, as she was at that age. As I probably was, for that matter, when I was four. As most of us were. And why not? Language makes a promise, when we first begin to speak it—a promise that everything will come together: our thoughts, our words, our universe. "The unity of truth," the medieval philosophers called it, and what they were describing is the feeling we sometimes have that the world is trying to make sense for us. The beauty of things, their goodness, their sheer existence: Our ideas hunger to be true, our words strain to enlighten, and reality—the pure essence of things— longs to be thought and said.

It's tricky, this kind of high metaphysics, and maybe the philosophers were wrong about it all. Or maybe the unity of truth makes sense only when cast up to the level of God himself. There's a reason, after all, that the Gospel of John begins the way it does: *In the beginning was the Word, and the Word was with God, and the Word was God.* Oxen kneeling, fearful shepherds, the swirl of angels—even the gold and frankincense and myrrh the Wise Men bring: all those famous Christmas scenes derive from passages elsewhere in the Bible. John opens only with the incomprehensible unity of truth. With the impossible moment when speech and thought and reality merged in a newborn child. With the first Christmas, there in Bethlehem, beneath a star, when *the Word was made flesh, and dwelt among us.*

Still, the experience of unity—that feeling I've called "the enchantment of the world at Christmas": it has at least a metaphor in the way that language wants to mean more than just its definitions. I'm doing something odd, I know, when I talk about what words *want* to do, as though they were living things: obstinate and willful creatures, trotting along with purposes and principles all their own.

But you can feel what I mean in Christmas words if you loosen the reins a little and let them find their own way home, like horses through the snow. *Yule* and *gladsome, hark* and *dayspring, Noël* and *wassail*: there's a surprising amount of language we know—old vocabulary that remains in the common wordstock, wrapped like presents under the tree—only because Christmas preserves it for us. And all those words are strange, shivery things, richer than they have to be.

Remember the old jingle about how Christmas is coming and the goose is getting fat? Even out on the South Dakota prairie, I learned it very young—as you probably did, wherever you grew up, for the song is essentially a nursery rhyme. *Please put a penny in the old man's hat,* it begs. But *If you haven't got a penny, a ha'penny will do. / If you haven't got a ha'penny, then God bless you!* And the coin isn't just some antique half-penny piece from England, discontinued decades ago. Because of that Christmas song, because of the enchantment of language, the word *ha'penny* is also a lesson: a morality tale about poverty and charity and God's love for the poor and what the yuletide season calls us to remember. What the gladsome tidings bring. What the herald angels sing, if only we—ah, yes, of course. You know how the carol goes: if only we hearken unto them.

II

LANGUAGE IS ALL we have, really, with which to grasp the world. Oh, we can measure things, and theorize about them, and contemplate their moving parts; break up the universe with picks and sledgehammers, for that matter, and try to cobble it together again when we're done. "Bash to fit, and paint to cover," as my father's friend, the fast-talking Sam Sheridan, used to say about assembling anything mechanical while I worked with him at the California gold mine. But the point is that he had to *say* it. When you get down to the root, words are how we treat the world: organizing, manipulating, adjusting. Words are how we work.

And it may be that those words are merely tools—implements we fashion for ordinary purposes, like cavemen chipping away at flint: hammering out the rough meanings and crude messages we need for getting on with our lives. But they do seem to end up a lot noisier than they need to be, don't they? They bubble and pop as we use them. They grind against one another; they squeak and growl.

There is, in truth, an evanescence to language, and we all knew it when we were young. We'd watch the drift of words through the air like snow, staring out the living room window at the storm as we knelt on the sofa cushions, our chins propped on the sofa back. We'd bundle up and run out in the cold to catch them on our tongues. We'd roll in the new-fallen stuff, sweeping out the clean shapes of angel figures on a white lawn. We'd pack words down to icy globes between our mittens and fling them at stoplights and fence posts and school-crossing signs—at the icicles that drooped from a neighbor's eaves, too, until the Christmas that Scooter, the boy from down Elizabeth Street, and I broke Mr. Wilson's attic window and we fled to hide behind the snow-filled lilacs, half hysterical with laughter, half terrified.

I remember how cold the air had grown, there in Pierre that night, shivering inside my parka as my mother sent me back to Mr. Wilson's with my allowance money to apologize. At what age do we stop carrying coins in our mittens? Not that I needed money often, but I always held my cash there when I did, and the quarters from my piggy bank felt hot and strange against my palm. Those red mittens— I'd forgotten all about them, but suddenly I can see them again in my mind, exactly as they were: a gray stripe zigzagging across the backs, and my mother had sewn a long piece of green yarn that ran up one sleeve, across the back, and down the opposite sleeve to attach them to each other. I'd shake the mittens off and let them dangle when I wanted to make a really smooth snowball, but that night they were still cold and damp from the afternoon.

I remember the sharp squeak of the snow beneath my black rubber overshoes, how it wouldn't pack anymore: the powdery flakes so much drier and harder once the sun had set. And I remember hesitating for minutes, there in the freezing dark on the front walk of the house next to Mr. Wilson's— just outside the reach of his porch light—while I tried to think what to say. While I tried to find the words to use.

What makes a particular bit of language special, what supplies it with the voltage of extra meaning, isn't always its shared meaning. Sometimes otherwise casual words and phrases become electric through an experience, through being part of a story. The winter I was . . . well, now, I'm not exactly sure how old I was. Twelve, maybe, or thirteen when I had the paper route. And the only problem with delivering newspapers was Mrs. Johansen, the woman who always complained. *Always* complained. She'd carp about the newsprint smearing. She'd whine that I had folded the paper wrong. She'd nag that I was late.

Never mind that I was delivering to all her neighbors; she just *knew* that some of them, most of them, every one of them, were waiting for a chance to steal her newspaper, and she'd make me wedge the paper—folded in thirds—between her door handle and the jamb to keep it safe. Which was fine on a Saturday. But who could get a fat Friday edition into that narrow space? So every time I fumbled at the door, I'd hear her.

Actually, no, not every time. Memory is an unreliable guide, at best, exaggerating a few occasions into a universal experience. Still, often enough, she'd be up at six in the morning: a hatchet-thin woman with a glare and a terry-cloth bathrobe, snatching open the door to catch me, and I'd mumble something while she snarled that her paper hadn't been delivered earlier, folded just the way she liked. I tried rearranging my route to reach her at different times, but it didn't matter. She was always there, and she hated me, and I hated her as I trudged through the snow. It was dark and cold, those winter mornings: cold enough that the snow would scrunch beneath my boots, and I'd leave a trail of sharp footprints in the new snow across the lawns and unshoveled sidewalks. Until I got to Mrs. Johansen's house.

Now, this is a Christmas story—a memory that came back to me the other day as I swept the snow off my own porch in our Black Hills town of Hot Springs. It's common to say that smell is the most evocative of senses, but the fact is not less true for all that. Some scent I caught as I worked seemed to fish down in the ice ponds of memory and pull up, almost intact, the fragrance of old Christmas wreaths on the doors of dark houses. The smell of fresh ink, just before dawn. The rich ozone aroma of diesel exhaust from the school bus warming up in a snowy parking lot. The snow, for that matter.

In those days, snow itself seemed to have a scent; it made the world smell different: crisper, cleaner, sharper.

So maybe it was only the winter air—the redolence of snow—here in adulthood that brought back to mind, for the first time in years, the bitterness of Mrs. Johansen and the Christmas morning I paused in dread outside her house on my predawn paper route. But I had presents waiting back home, calling from beneath the tree for the family to wake and open them, and church to attend, and relatives coming for a breakfast of eggs and toast and that awful grapefruit a cousin always sent a case of in December, which I had to drown in sugar to get down, and candles and carols and all the rest. And so, at last, I climbed up to her unswept porch to cram her paper in the doorway. And of course it wouldn't fold easily in my cold hands, and of course that gave her time to reach the door before I could get away, and there she was, glowering at me, in a brown bathrobe with cotton slippers on her feet.

You know how houses sometimes have a living odor? Not foul, exactly. Just a sour taint, as though its residents don't open the doors and windows often enough. That's the smell I remember, as Mrs. Johansen stood there on Christmas morning. She tore the paper from my hands, glared for a second, and then shoved at me a large, round, pink tin of Almond Roca candy, snatched up from the entryway table. "For you," she muttered. "For Christmas." And she pushed shut the door.

I don't know, maybe she had places to go, people to visit. For that matter, maybe she had friends and family coming over, although it seemed unlikely. Almost alone on the block, her house had no decorations. The tin wasn't wrapped, and there was no card or bow, but somehow she had gathered herself enough to go out and buy me a present, because— because I was in her life, I suppose, and she maybe didn't have many people in her life, and it was the Christmas season when we are called to imagine a different way for ourselves, and . . . but no, I've never known, for sure, and I know that a better person would have found out. A better person than I was, in those days. A better person than I am, now.

That suddenly returning memory of Mrs. Johansen this year made me realize, while I swept my own porch, that I hadn't seen Almond Roca for sale in years. So I wrote to ask if it was still being made—and promptly got back in the mail four pink tins of the stuff, from the head of the Brown & Haley candy company off in Tacoma, Washington. It tasted fine, but back when I was twelve or thirteen, as I walked home in the cold predawn, with the empty canvas newspaper bag bumping against my back, the candy seemed something more than fine. It was crunchy, wrapped in little individual wrappers, and it smelled like toffee and roasted nuts and almond extract. It smelled, in truth, like Christmas.

And those words, *Almond Roca*: They have for me, still, an extended sense about them—an extra charge in the electricity of language. They mean, like so many words, just a little bit more than they have to.

III

IT'S NOT ONLY the language of Christmas that works this way, although, in the elaborate analogy I'm building here, the shimmer of Christmas words makes them figures—"seasonable tokens," in Charles Dickens's marvelous phrase—for the inexpressible Word they try so hard to express. But ordinary language, the everyday stuff of speech, can also have that strange gleam of something extra.

If you think about it, my daughter, Faith, was right, back in Washington when she was four—not just about her file cabinet stairway not being a good idea but even about language: *Thwart* really is a good word. Roll it around a little in your mouth, and you'll know what I mean: *thwart, thwarted, athwart.* A kind of satisfaction lives in such words—a unity, a completion. *Skirt, scalp, drab, buckle, sneaker, twist,* and *jumble. Squeamish,* for that matter. They have a savor, a taste, and they seem to resound with their own truthfulness. More like proper nouns than merely words, they try to match the things they name.

I'd attempt to describe just how enjoyable words can be—their sheer wordiness, all weird and wonderful—but I'm not sure I have to. The jewelers I'd walk by while we lived in New York, arguing over carats and bezels and cabochons; the carpenters I worked with in Utah, talking about rabbets and routers and bradawls; the farmers we'd visit as children, out on the plains, pointing to scythes and cultivators and moldboard plows: everybody revels in the technical vocabulary of their professions (lawyers maybe a little too much). When I was a child, I would climb the river buttes near Pierre with my grandmother, listening as she happily told me the names of the plants and birds we'd see. Years later, in the green rooms of Washington, I would sit with the professional chatterers—the talking heads who populate the television talk shows—and sense the pleasure they took in pronouncing the titles of obscure federal agencies. The delight that people take in words is all around us, all the time. Eavesdrop a little, and you can hear it in the supermarkets and hardware stores, in the nursing homes and grade schools.

Think of *pickle, gloomy, portly, curmudgeon*—just saying them aloud is a joy, as they loop back on themselves to close the circle of meaning with their own sound. Admittedly, some of this effect comes from onomatopoeia: words that echo the noise they name. *Hiccup,* for instance, and *zip.* The animal cries of *quack* and *oink* and *howl.* The mechanical noises of *click* and *clack* and *clank.* Chickadees, cuckoos, and whip-poor-wills all get their names this way. Whooping cranes, as well, and when I was little, I pictured them as sickly birds, somehow akin to whooping cough.

And yet, that word *akin*—that's a good word, too, even though it lacks the near-onomatopoeia of *percussion* and *lullaby,* or the picture-drawing of things like *clickety-clack* and *gobble.* The words I'm thinking of are the ones that, for whatever reason, feel right when we say them: accurate expressions of themselves. *Apple,* for instance, has always seemed a perfect name, a crisp and tanged and ruddy word. *Jab* and *fluffy* and *sneer,* each of them true in a way that lies beyond logic. *Verbose* has always struck me as a strangely verbose word. *Peppy* has that perky, energetic sound it needs. And never was there a word more supercilious than *supercilious* or more lethargic than *lethargic.*

Ethereal is one of these, isn't it? All ethereal and airy. *Rapier, swashbuckler, erstwhile, spume*—true of themselves, every one. Teach them to a child, and you'll soon grow sick of it, for they're the kind of words that, once learned, children love to pronounce, over and over and over. *Reverberation* reverberates, and *jingle* jingles. A friend insists that *machination* is a word that tells you all about its sneaky, Machiavellian self, and *sporadic* has something patchy and intermittent in the taste as you say it.

Odd. Now there's a word that says just what it means. *Dwindle* wants to fade away even while you're saying it. And surely *splendiferous* is right for itself, expressing its own hollow pomposity. For that matter, isn't *hollow* a little hollow, with the sound of a hole at its center? Maybe that's just my imagination, but you always know where you are with words like *dreary* and *gossip* and *gut* and *bludgeon*. *Gargoyle* sounds like a word that knows just what it is. *Snake* and *swoop* and *spew* all reach back to gnaw on themselves. They have their poetry built into them. They reach up toward the light that makes our Christmas words so glittery. They're what all language wants to be, when it grows up.

IV

EXCEPT, OF COURSE, that words don't grow up. Not exactly. It's more that, sometimes, we grow into them, like those school clothes my mother would make or buy at the end of summer: turtlenecks and corduroy pants that flopped around our wrists and ankles every September because she wanted to leave us room to grow.

The childish glimmer, the glamour, of words proves . . . well, no, it doesn't *prove* anything. But it hints, at least, that words contain more than dictionaries and grammar guides say they do. If we can't name it the Proof from Poetry, we can at least call it the Argument from Poetry—for the sparkle of words on the outside suggests they have a light on the inside, and the extra verbal *oomph* we sensed when we were young is an intimation of the extra content we might grasp as we grow older. That first innocence of language we knew as children, in other words, points toward a second innocence we could know as adults—a kind of fulfillment of words, waiting for us far off in the unity of truth.

The transition is hard to describe, partly, I think, because it's such a hard transition to live. There's a time between, a sort of adolescent moment, when the outward light of words has faded and the inward light has not yet broken through. Old place names, moral judgments, technical terms; everyday speech, for that matter: All of it can begin to sound lifeless and dull. Even good words like *thwart*: chipped flint to skin a rough beast and nothing more.

And yet, think of *wreaths* and *holly, fruitcakes* and *mistletoe*. *St. Nick* and Scrooge's *humbug,* as far as that goes. *Joseph* and *Mary*. *Ornaments* and *snowflakes* and *magi*. Something more than just happenstance lives in these Christmas words—something more than the simple task of expressing a seasonal meaning. They don't exactly name things, around Christmas. They don't even refer to ideas, down at the root. Christmas is true as poetry—words speaking, each to each—long before it's true as fact. Christmas is a time when language has been let alone to do what it really wants to do. And what it wants is both to glitter with iridescence and to glow with purpose. What language wants, most of all, is to be fleshed with meaning.

Look, here's a story I heard out on the South Dakota plains where I grew up. One of my father's friends told it to me, on a visit home to Pierre with my daughter, and I seem to recall my grandmother telling a version of it as well. The occasion I remember best, however, was near Christmas, one of those winters when I was young. There was something I wanted to do, some trip I wanted to make, and my parents wouldn't let me. So I responded the way adolescents usually respond: by glowering, sniping away in sarcastic comments, affecting exhaustion, and being unpleasant in the way only a teenager can manage. At last, having finally had enough of it, my great-aunt ordered me to get my coat and mittens and meet her outside.

I found her in front, with the car running, and she took me down in silence to the river, just below the dam, where the Missouri runs in open water all winter between its cold banks. The defroster blew up against the windshield, barely keeping out the cold as the car idled, and I waited and waited, crunched down in protest, dreading the lecture I was sure she was about to give. But she sat there for a long while, looking out at the river, minute after minute, until at last she sighed and began:

"You know Waller Johnson, don't you? The rancher from out toward Philip. Your father has done some legal work for him, over the years. Lord, I remember Waller when he was young. A big, good-looking boy off the range. Your great-grandfather helped bring him to Pierre, found him a place to stay during the school year—partly so he could finish high school, but mostly, I think, so he could play baseball and Pierre could beat Yankton. Charlie loved baseball.

"I want to tell you a story about him. Back in the

early 1930s, his mother and father died, the mortgage payments stopped, and the Land Bank repossessed the ranch. Waller must have been seventeen or eighteen in those days. But somehow he talked the Land Bank into letting him try to bring the herd to market. We gave him what help we could, but those were hard times all over, and no one thought he could do it—not with four younger brothers and sisters to feed at the same time.

"But he was a tough young man. He kept the herd together through the winter, fattened the cattle up, sold them, and reclaimed the ranch. Then he put his brothers and sisters through school, and saw them settled, here and there. Finally Waller settled down himself, marrying a girl named Nancy Trike from, oh, I don't know—Spearfish, maybe. I remember she was a pretty thing, but thin and a little sickly.

"One winter—it must have been '42 or '43, during the war, anyway—their furnace broke down, in the middle of a blizzard, and their baby began running a fever."

She watched the water as it poured past, skinned with ice along the edge. "You're too young to know what it was like in those days," she said. "Most of the ranches didn't have electricity. Hardly any had plumbing. The roads were bad, and the nearest doctor was at the hospital in Pierre, maybe fifty miles away. The adults could have built a fire, cuddled up for warmth, and outlasted the storm. But the baby was sick, and they didn't think he would make it through the cold. So Waller and Nancy loaded up the car with blankets and coats they'd warmed in the oven, and started off through the snow to Pierre.

"It took them four, almost five, hours to make that drive. The blizzard was pounding down from the north, swirling across the prairie the way it does. If they missed the road or slid off into a gully, they would die—not just the baby, but all three of them, left there frozen until somebody came along and found them.

"I want you to picture this—really see it, as clearly as you can: the blinding snow, that old car creeping along the icy road, the sick child wrapped up between them, Waller and Nancy straining to watch the road, rubbing their breath off the windows—knowing they might be killed but knowing they had to try."

"Why didn't they stay at the ranch?" I asked, growing colder and more confused every minute we sat there in her car by the river. "I mean, that way, at least two of them would survive. If they really thought they weren't going to make it, then they were just throwing themselves away."

"They really *did* think they weren't going to make it," she answered. "But they had to do it anyway. It wasn't a choice. It wasn't something to be added up, weighing their lives against the baby's. They couldn't choose their own survival against a chance of his, however small." She turned to me, and her face was hard with something I couldn't quite understand. "And do you see why? It's because they were parents. And that's what the word *parent* means. They had already given up their lives for that child's, from the moment he was born."

She sighed again and looked back out at the river. "In that blizzard, the bill finally came due, and they had to pay it   the way you will pay it, when your time comes. The way your mother and father will pay it, when they have to. That's what I want you to remember the next time you're angry with them, the next time you want to scream because they won't let you do something, the next time you feel as though nobody understands how grown up you've become."

She glanced over at me and smiled, pulling the cloth sleeve of her coat up over her hand to wipe the windshield. "Let's go," she said. "It's time to get back home."

Years later, I came to see my great-aunt's story as the answer to utilitarianism and the ethics of calculation, the solution to those "lifeboat cases" we were supposed to ponder in freshman philosophy classes. But at the time I knew only that she was trying, in her way, to let me in on the secret of adulthood, the mystery and the trick of it. She was explaining, as best as she could, the Argument from Poetry: there is a meaning to certain words—their deepest, truest inwardness, their moral content— that comes clear only with experience. *Parent, birth, Christmas, child, God*: these are big words, capacious things that dwarf the mind that tries to grasp them. And though we may learn their dictionary meanings while we're young, they leave us room to grow. Lots and lots of room to grow.

V

LITTLE LORD JESUS no crying he makes and *We three kings of Orient are*—to say nothing of *if thou knowst it telling*: Have you ever observed just how peculiar the grammar and syntax of Christmas carols can be? Or maybe that should run *The songs of*

Christmas, noticed thou, / the strangeness filled with are—and how?

The oddest may be "God Rest Ye Merry Gentlemen," whose phrasings are now so alien that even the first line gets regularly mangled—punctuated (and sung) as *God rest ye, merry gentlemen,* which suggests the gentlemen have made so merry that God needs to send them sleep, saving us from their wassailed warbling through the streets. The original meaning was "rest" in the sense of "keep," requiring the comma in a different place: *God rest ye merry, gentlemen*—a prayer that God keep joy in the hearts of men. Not that this stops them from spiking the eggnog at the office party, but it might lessen the next day's hangover.

Meanwhile, a later verse tells us that a blessèd angel came and *unto certain shepherds / brought tidings of the same.* What same? *How that in Bethlehem was born / the Son of God by name,* of course, and there's something wonderful about that line. It's incompetent poetry, filler to make a rhyme of the most naive sort—*by name,* forsooth—and it's really quite charming, in its way.

Even stranger is the moment when we're told that the newborn babe was laid within a manger—*the which his Mother Mary / did nothing take in scorn.* You'd think that would create some *which–witch* confusion for modern singers, but not even children hesitate at the line. English doesn't use *the which* as a construction much anymore. Still, when carolers sing it out, the phrase seems to come from the authentic heart of the language. It feels right, somehow. It feels old.

That feeling of antiquity, that power to appear traditional, remains a requirement of the music—even though Christmas carols are essentially a Victorian invention. Not that people didn't sing seasonal songs before the nineteenth century: Ever since St. Augustine first came to Canterbury to convert the nation, England has been full of local hymns and carols, from "Christus Est Natus" to "The Cherry Tree Carol." But the Victorians were the ones who systematized it all (especially Henry Ramsden Bramley and John Stainer, with their 1871 songbook *Christmas Carols New and Old*). The universal Christmas canon they established contained some genuinely older songs: "The First Nowell," for instance, and the Wesleyan "Hark, the Herald Angels Sing." Much of what the Victorians did, however, was write new songs they tried to make sound old.

The result was often silly, to say the least: the pointless "thees" and "thous," the pretentiously archaic syntax, the inversions and padding for rhyme. Nonetheless, every year, one or another of those carols catches me and hauls me in. The first Christmas song usually steals into town right after Thanksgiving, like the gentle plink that signals a cloudburst, and within days the deluge is inescapable: the office elevators and the street corners and the stores awash in holiday music. Beginning as an unwelcome reminder of just how fast Christmas is coming, the ceaseless tintinnabulation of those old familiar anthems quickly grows almost unbearable: as cloying as silver bells jangling endlessly in the middle distance.

I've never known a world without recorded Christmas carols. When I was young, my sisters and I would dig out our parents' scratchy discs of Joan Baez trilling away at "O Come, O Come, Emmanuel" and Burl Ives growling out "The Friendly Beasts" and Peter, Paul, and Mary harmonizing a song whose name I can't remember, but it was about a shivering boy who shares his only piece of bread with a gray-haired lady on Christmas Eve, and we used to play it over and over again on the hi-fi in the basement.

Ever since the voice of Enrico Caruso was first pressed on a scratchy, one-sided 78 rpm record for Mr. Edison's new gramophone machine, nearly every musical performer has felt compelled to issue a Christmas album, and the sheer bulk of that music adds up to more than anyone could listen to in a thousand holidays. The big three of the season—

Bing Crosby, Frank Sinatra, and Nat King Cole—
remain perennial best sellers, while Elvis Presley's
holiday collections and the Mormon Tabernacle
Choir's recordings hold their own. But the music
stores' discount bins tumble together Mantovani
and the Nitty Gritty Dirt Band, Tony Bennett and
the Vienna Boys Choir, *Paul Revere and the Raiders Sing the Season* and *The Amazing Zamfir Plays Carols on His Pan Pipes*—together with Christmas
anthologies from Muzak, Motown, the Metropolitan Opera, and the Grand Ole Opry.

I once bought a version of a carol—I think it
was supposed to be "Good King Wenceslas"—
performed on bagpipes, just to hear what it sounded
like. Not good, is the answer. By itself, it was enough
to make all the Whos down in Whoville cheer that
the Grinch stole their Christmas. But most of the
traditional songs are traditional for a reason: they're
sturdy enough to stand up to almost anything the
yuletide pits against them—Herb Alpert and the
Tijuana Brass, or a grade-school Christmas recital,

or even my own adventures in shower singing. (I pride myself on knowing Christmas carols' more rarely sung verses—the bit about thorn-infestation in "Joy to the World," for instance—and one of the nice things about living now in the bigger spaces of South Dakota is that I can get all the way to those grimmer parts of holiday tunes without my wife knocking on the door to say the neighbors are complaining. Again.) Even when my sisters and I were children, the innumerable Christmas renditions would blend together until Don Ho's *'Mele Kalikimaka' is the thing to say / on a bright Hawaiian Christmas Day* sounded just like Nat King Cole's *'Buon Natale' in Italy / means a Merry Christmas to you.*

And yet, good or bad, distinct or indistinct, a carol snares me every year and tumbles me down—down into that Christmas world of time turned somehow less ephemeral: weightier, denser, and more real; a world where symbols are not just symbols anymore. One year it was a boy soprano singing "Once in Royal David's City." Another year, a melancholy country-western recording of "God Rest Ye Merry Gentleman," rendered in a minor key. Another year, an a cappella version of "See, Amid the Winter's Snow."

I can find little similarity in the passing years' triggers of Christmas, except perhaps that they usually come during the carols' less-familiar second or third verses, at a line with some explicit Christian piety and heft. *Mild, he lays his glory by, / Born that man no more may die,* I heard in "Hark, the Herald Angels Sing" on the car radio as I drove home one Christmas season, and home was newly bathed in that old, familiar light. *Yet in thy dark streets shineth / The everlasting Light* from "O Little Town of Bethlehem," the carolers sang another year on the steps of a nursing home as I walked by, and it rose, and it rose, and it rose like a torrent. And down in the flood, I was washed away.

Every year, Christmas begins for me with the dance of words, and those words, often enough, arrive first in the lyrics of carols. Late one night when she was four—there in the Christmas season, the evening after her filing cabinet misadventure—I took my daughter in my arms and hummed for her the old, old songs. There is a world where shepherds still keep watch over their flocks by night. There is a world where oxen still kneel at midnight in their straw. There is a world where Wenceslas still trudges through the winter snow.

There is a world, I whispered in her sleepy hair. There is a world where still.

Chapter 3

Comfort and Joy

The brightness of the shops where holly sprigs and berries crackled in the lamp heat of the windows, made pale faces ruddy as they passed. Poulterers' and grocers' trades became a splendid joke; a glorious pageant, with which it was next to impossible to believe that such dull principles as bargain and sale had anything to do.

—*A CHRISTMAS CAROL*

I

CHRISTMAS IS COMING, my daughter sang in that piercing, glass-shattering treble of small girls. *Christmas is coming, my father's getting fat. / Please put a penny in the old man's hat.* So I gave her a stern and serious lecture about honoring her parents, while I swung her up in the air and dropped her, giggling and squealing, with an *oomph* on the living room sofa.

In truth, I could have used the penny. And somewhere in the run from Halloween's candy to Thanksgiving's sage-and-bread stuffing to the Christmas goose, the old man did manage to get as fat. All domestic discipline went up the chimney with the letter to Santa Claus. The brakes came off the sled, and the household's financial, dietary, and even—as my daughter's open teasing of her father suggests—parental controls vanished. Probably in the bright flash that sent me out to buy three new strands of Christmas tree lights and new batteries for the smoke detector as our old lights announced their retirement in a fine cascade of sparks and the stench of charring plastic.

"Did we leave that candy dish in storage?" I asked in exasperation, as I performed the annual unpacking of the annual implements of annual Christmas decoration. "You remember, the glass one my grandmother gave us. I always use it for the candies my cousin sends." And with endless patience, Lorena answered that no, it isn't in storage, because I had broken it two years before, when I tripped on the scattered parts of the train set I'd insisted any daughter would love for a present. That was the tumble, Lorena reminded me, in which I'd broken a lamp, a side table, and a pair of the Christmas mugs my mother gave us. Plus the candy dish and a household rule about not using certain expletives in front of children.

Ah, yes, that Christmas. Other people seem to remember Christmases by what they received or what they gave: a Christmas of presents. I tend to mark particular years by what we lost: a Christmas of broken things. The year the tree toppled and smashed the glass ornaments Lorena's sister sent from Egypt. The year a log rolled out of the fireplace and singed a trail across the living room rug. The year I smiled down from the ladder as my toddler daughter, wide-eyed with wonder, tried to hand up to me the angel we put atop the tree. I seem to remember she learned a few new words that Christmas, as well.

Tidings of comfort and joy, the carol proclaims. And joy there certainly is. But comfort? That has always seemed to me a slightly skewed theology about Christ's Nativity, at least in the modern sense of the word *comfort,* and anyway, it isn't true. I had this insight one morning this year as I knelt on the floor, trying to brush out of the rug the tiny slivers of silvered glass from the latest broken ornament. I cut myself, of course, because, well, that's what those ornaments are for, aren't they? I mean, not actually for physical injury, although the annual wounds are probably a secondary design feature. But surely some discomfort is part of the season—if only to remind us to look for Christmas joy rather than Christmas comfort. These are, after all, different things. Comfort, as we use the word these days, is an aspiration that can never be fulfilled short of the grave, for each new comfort creates its discomforts, which need in turn new comforts in an never-ending cycle. And, anyway, the desire for comfort is the hunger for a condition, a state.

But joy—joy is an activity, isn't it? Joy is something we do, or at least something we feel while we are up and doing. There's probably not a lot of mileage to be gained by trying to spread tidings of discomfort and joy. And, in truth, a little comfort at Christmas would be a welcome change from the usual run of breakage and spoilage. But I'll take the joy, since that seems to be what is chiefly on offer.

II

THE TROUBLE WITH writing about all this is Charles Dickens. He bestrides the season's literature like a Christmas colossus—and doesn't that word *bestride* capture something of the Victorian feeling to which he gave expression? Although maybe it's better to think of him as the torrent of a raging river. (He loved that, too, in his writing: shifting metaphors like a conjurer, so fast you never quite see what happens to the playing card he will shortly make appear in your coat pocket.)

Anyway, say you're drifting in your canoe down the Christmas stream—the pines dusted with snow along the banks, the scenes of your childhood reflected in the play of the winter sun on the water, the divine meaning of the holiday looming like the canyon cliffs above you. And you see an interesting creek or backwater off to the side, something that looks worth exploring. So you start to row over, only to discover that the current has got you. There's this nice little calm place near the bank, and you're paddling like a madman to reach it, but the surge of the water doesn't want to let you go. It's taken hold, good and hard, and no matter how much you fight, you can't escape being pulled down the main channel of the river. And over the waterfall.

That's Dickens: the river, and probably the waterfall, as well. I sometimes attempt to write the

way he did, to do the Dickensian dance of Christmas, but I end up only with passages like this:

Ah, Christmas time, that fecund moment most
welcome in the bleak of bitter winter! Ah, Advent
days, so rich, so ripe, so opulent in the golden light
of charity, while like a pall of poverty the hoary
frost and thin-crust snow lie hard upon the cold-
pressed earth! Ah, Yuletide, when for the briefest
instant in the rush of loud and cruel commerce—
alas, so brief!—all the earth may pause and speak
again of gentle things in gentle accents!

The sentimental glop of that prose isn't really
Dickens. Oh, he was plenty sentimental, but when
you attempt to match it, to be sentimental in the way
he was, you flounder just as his Victorian imitators
did. Not that I blame them for trying to copy his
success. We all get pulled down the river, one way
or another. Unfortunately, only Dickens survives it,
and before long the sentimentality of the imitation

sickens even the paper on which it's written and my abused pencil explodes in a shower of angry sparks, red and green to match the season. "Jeeves was in the other room hanging holly," as P. G. Wodehouse once wrote in antidote, "for Christmas would soon be at our throats."

In truth, Wodehouse found his own share of corniness as an author, and anyway, on the topics of sentimentality and antisentimentality, someone like G. K. Chesterton is probably a better model— for he would have pointed out that a thing isn't necessarily false just because it's wrought with easy emotion. Chesterton is another of the irresistible currents for writers, especially for those of us who want to make a theological point in our writing. (And something more than *especially* for those of us who want to use Christmas to make that theological point.) You start thinking in a Chestertonian way about Christmas, and you end up producing imitations like this:

The distaste for sentimentality begins as a revolt against false feeling, and it finishes as a rebellion against all feeling. It starts as our refusal to be deceived by a coat of paint, and it ends as our refusal to use any paint at all. It opens as a wise man's ability to see fool's gold, and it concludes as a fool's inability to see real gold.

For on this point, we dare not be mistaken: Christmas is the real gold, and all the sentimentality with which we gild a thing already golden, all the evergreens with which we decorate a thing already green, all the holly boughs with which we mark a thing already holy—all these are not some vain attempt to mask the truth. They are, rather, the tribute that sentiment will always try to pay to true things, on the same principle by which a wife chooses the prettiest wrapping paper for her husband's most expensive gift on Christmas morning.

What need had the King of Kings—what

need had a newborn child in a cattle shed—for the awful oblation of gold and frankincense and myrrh laid before him by the Wise Men? And yet those men were wise, as we are wisest only in our greatest foolishness.

Something in the holiday seems to wring out of me this kind of fake-Chestertonian stuff: every sentence an aphorism, eased along by alliteration, until the words clot up in a giant Christmas pudding that subsides with a half-baked sigh as it cools upon the table. All the way back in 1920, F. Scott Fitzgerald had a character in one of his novels complain, "I'm sick of Chesterton," and you know what he means. From January to November, Chesterton's wordy style may go down easy. But around Christmas, while the streets ring with Salvation Army bells and the elevators buzz with Muzaked carols, it's just too much. Just too much.

And yet . . . well, and yet, how are we to help

ourselves? Every one of those jingling bells and jangling carols awakens some remembrance, haunting the middle distance of a mind that had thought itself too mature to be moved again by mere memory. With his memoir *A Child's Christmas in Wales,* the poet Dylan Thomas drew the template for this kind of childhood-describing prose, and his voice, too, is an ever-present pull on everyone who wants to write about the season:

> The snows of my childhood Christmases drift against the house in Pierre, one year's memories piled on another's, until it seems my family must have lived beneath a dome of ice, an igloo of those years arched above us, lit with a seal-oil lamp. And we children, proper little Eskimos as we always wanted to be, would be awakened on those winter mornings by our mother—who fed us on polar-bear porridge, wrapped us in pale fox furs, and sent us out to hunt the arctic wastes,

searching for walruses, narwhale tusks, and lost explorers in need of directions. Turn left at Mr. Wilson's house on the corner, we planned to tell them, then straight on to the pole.

Penguins, too, somehow dwelt among us, squawking loudly that they had no business this far north, in that world of imagination now melted, with all its abominable snowmen and angels cast by lying on our backs and waving our arms in the snow, by the hot glare of the passing years. But the penguins did belong there, as all bright, alive, exotic things belonged, for this was Christmas, and Christmas itself was bright, alive, and exotic in the cold: burning like a flame in those days now down beneath the snow. And there were aunts and uncles and carols and candies and the hushed, sleepy mystery as we walked back from midnight church that made my sister ask, "It really is real, isn't it?" And I said yes, for it was, and really, it still is, deep in the drifts of memory.

Of course, after a bout of attempting this Dylan Thomasy writing—all run-on sentences and modifiers misplacedly modifying—I find myself wanting to take up Ernest Hemingway in self-defense. Short sentences. Nothing but short sentences.

But what's left? There isn't a style or a voice we can use to write about Christmas that isn't already hackneyed or overused or trite. And yet, in that fact itself may lie the answer—especially the answer Charles Dickens found in stories like *A Christmas Carol,* for what Dickens understood is that Christmas would eat us up, if it could. It would absorb everything around it, pull everything into its vortex. And our best chance of getting through it in one piece may be simply to surrender. Surrender to the torrent of the season. Surrender to the flood of feeling. Surrender to the sentimentality.

Surrender to Dickens, for that matter, and let Scrooge and Tiny Tim and all the rest have their day.

III

IT'S ALMOST IMPOSSIBLE not to know how *A Christmas Carol* opens: "Marley was dead: to begin with. There is no doubt whatever about that." The book has been filmed at least forty-two times and dramatized for the stage in dozens of versions— the first almost immediately after its publication in 1843, a pirated play that Dickens spent £700 to fight before he won an uncollectible judgment against its producers (and thereby found material for the great legal case of *Jarndyce and Jarndyce,* which lies at the center of his novel *Bleak House,* but that's another story). "Old Marley was as dead as a door-nail," the first paragraph of *A Christmas Carol* ends, as nearly everyone remembers.

But who recollects how the second paragraph runs? "Mind! I don't mean to say that I know, of my own knowledge, what there is particularly dead about a door-nail. I might have been inclined, my-self, to regard a coffin-nail as the deadest piece of ironmongery in the trade. But the wisdom of our ancestors is in the simile; and my unhallowed hands shall not disturb it, or the Country's done for. You will therefore permit me to repeat, emphatically, that Marley was as dead as a door-nail." You don't get much of that narrator's voice in the films we've all seen, over and over, every Christmas. You don't get the wordiness or the facetiousness. You don't get the hallucinogenic animation of inanimate objects. You don't get the comedy running over and under the sentimentality. You don't get the manic speed, or the almost insane energy, or the sheer delight in writing down words. You may get the story, but you don't get Dickens.

Which is a shame, since the story, taken by itself, is something of a mess. Not that we're much bothered by the fact—and something about the success of Dickens's art is revealed by the way we don't demand coherence from the plot. John Forster (Dickens's friend, unofficial agent, and biographer) once described the author as taking a "secret delight" in giving "a higher form" to nursery stories, and the fairy-tale quality is one of the things we feel immediately when we read *A Christmas Carol*. You would no more complain of its creaky plot than you would demand greater structural integrity from *Rumpelstiltskin* and *Cinderella*.

Still, the story line isn't what anyone would call tight. After talking to Marley's ghost until "past two" in the morning, Scrooge "went straight to bed, without undressing," only to awake to meet the Ghost of Christmas Past at midnight—two hours before he fell asleep and "clad but slightly in his slippers, dressing-gown, and nightcap." One feels a little mean-spirited objecting to the illogic of ghosts, but in *A Christmas Carol* they are made to behave more inconsistently than even ghosts deserve. Apparently nothing said by the Ghost of Christmas Yet to Come will come true. Bob Cratchit won't weep, "My little, little child!" at the memory of his dead son—for at the story's end, after Scrooge's reformation, we are assured that Tiny Tim "did not die." The new Scrooge will presumably meet his own death not alone, his bed curtains stolen from around his corpse, but surrounded by his adoring nephew Fred, Fred's wife, Fred's wife's plump sister, and even Tiny Tim, to whom he will become "a second father."

Even the Ghost of Christmas Present doesn't manage to get much right. The guests at Fred's Christmas party won't make fun of the absent Scrooge, because Scrooge will be there. The Cratchits won't have their little goose, "eked out by apple-sauce and mashed potatoes." They'll have instead the enormous "prize turkey" Scrooge has sent: "He never could have stood upon his legs, that bird. He would have snapped 'em short off in a minute, like sticks of sealing-wax." No wonder Bob Cratchit was a "full eighteen minutes and a half" late to work the next morning. The monstrous thing couldn't have been fully cooked until almost midnight. And didn't the Cratchits wonder where their meal had come from? For that matter, what is the poultry shop doing "half open" at six o'clock on Christmas morning—and why hasn't the poulterer already sold his prize bird, which, intended for some family's Christmas feast, is going to go bad in short order?

Meanwhile, the characters are as unconvincing as the plot. Scrooge was probably intended to be simply a placeholder for a fairy-tale's moral of conversion, but Dickens couldn't leave him alone. The miser ends up using far too much energy, taking far too much joy in being joyless. "If I could work my will . . . every idiot who goes about with 'Merry Christmas' on his lips, should be boiled with his own pudding, and buried with a stake of holly through his heart." "You may be an undigested bit of beef, a blot of mustard, a crumb of cheese, a fragment of an underdone potato," he says to Marley's ghost. "There's more of gravy than of grave about you, whatever you are!" He's ratcheted up too much to be a mere marker of villainy—just as, after his conversion, he's cranked up in insane glee: "Shaving was not an easy task, for his hand continued to shake very much; and shaving requires attention, even when you don't dance while you are at it."

But it isn't just Scrooge that Dickens can't leave alone. He can't leave *anything* alone—which is exactly what ends up making *A Christmas Carol* a triumph: the energy, the madness, the darting from thing to thing, the extravagance invested in every moment. The man's fiction contains thousands of named characters, and every single one of them has more poured into than necessary. Even the unnamed characters can't help becoming Dickensian. While Scrooge and the Ghost of Christmas Past watch old Fezziwig's party, "in came the cook, with her brother's particular friend, the milkman. In came the boy from over the way, who was suspected of not having board enough from his master, trying to hide himself behind the girl from next door but one."

Why do we have to know all this? Dickens is like some crazed magician, incapable of *not* transforming each thing that happens to catch his eye. In the obituary he wrote for the *Times* of London when Dickens died, his fellow novelist Anthony Trollope seemed to complain about how unfair it all was: every other writer has to bend his fiction to match reality, he observed, while reality bent itself to match Dickens; by the time Dickens was done creating a fictional orphan like Oliver Twist or a fictional miser like Scrooge, real orphans and misers had turned themselves into Dickensian characters. And that's what catches us all, really, as we read his books. I remember lying on my stomach when I was ten—stretched out on the bed down in the basement of the house in Pierre—reading *A Christmas Carol* for the first time, and I didn't stop, I couldn't stop, until the raging current of that Dickens river had washed me down to the end, banging me against the rocks along the way.

When *A Christmas Carol* was finished in 1843, Dickens and Forster "broke out" like madmen with (as he described it in a letter) "such dinings, such dancings, such conjurings, such blind-man's-bluffings, such theatre-goings, such kissings-out of old years and kissings-in of new ones [as] never took place in these parts before. . . . And if you could have seen me at the children's party at Macready's the other night . . ."

The prickly Victorian eccentric Jane Carlyle did see him at that party for the actor William Charles Macready's children. She hadn't slept well for weeks—hadn't slept at all the night before—and she was quarreling again with her husband, Thomas Carlyle. But once there, she found herself, like everyone else, caught up in the Dickensian world. "Dickens and Forster, above all, exerted themselves till the perspiration was pouring down and they seemed *drunk* with their efforts," she put it in her own letter about the party:

Only think of that excellent Dickens playing the *conjuror* for one whole hour—the *best* conjuror I ever saw. . . . Then the dancing . . . the gigantic Thackeray &c &c all capering like *Maenades!!* . . . *After supper* when we were all madder than ever with the pulling of crackers, the drinking of champagne, and the making of speeches; a universal country dance was proposed—and Forster *seizing me round the waist* whirled me into the thick of it, and *made* me dance!! like a person in the treadmill who must move forward or be crushed to death. Once I cried out, "Oh for the love of Heaven let me go! you are going to dash my brains out against the folding doors!" "Your *brains*!!" he answered, "who cares about their brains *here*? *Let them go!*"

The party rose "to something not unlike the *rape of the Sabines!*" and then Dickens carried Forster and Thackeray off to his house *"to finish the night there* and a *royal* night they would have of it

I fancy!" But Jane Carlyle went home instead to sleep—and sleep and sleep, her first healthy night in what felt to her like years.

There's some deep reflection in that scene, an image for the age in which they lived—and maybe an image for Christmas itself: The mad Victorian extrovert Charles Dickens, his best-known story just finished, gathering up everyone around him and animating them like puppets with his own Christmas energy. And in it, the mad Victorian introvert Jane Carlyle at last finding peace.

IV

"DICKENS DEAD? THEN will Father Christmas die, too?" asked a little girl in London on that summer day in 1870 when the great author slipped away. Or so, at least, the story is told, and if it seems believable, that's because Dickens created Christmas. Well, no, obviously he didn't *actually* create it. The great gift of God, descending in the flesh to be born in a cattle shed, did that work, almost two thousand years before. But Dickens is one of the people who opened the maw of the season and force-fed it on fruitcakes and sugarplums. Which has become a problem for us, yes?

Christmas was always something that would re-make the world, if it could. The intersection of the human and the divine must be, by its very nature, an attractor of meaning. Think of it as an enor-mous magnet, its lines of force rearranging every-thing around it like iron filings. Or a whirlwind in the desert, where all the nearby dunes are reshaped simply by its swirl. This is what powerful stories al-ways do, the effect of deep ideas: they colonize and expand, giving the old world a new order.

Sometimes the older insights and explanations disappear in the process, too contrary to survive the changed idea. Once Christianity spread in the old Celtic countries, even the unconverted Druids pretty much gave up the idea of stuffing human beings inside wicker baskets and burning them alive. Once the Norsemen had been baptized, they didn't entirely stop their Viking raiding, but they did admit they couldn't continue to drink from the skulls of their slaughtered enemies as a boast to Odin and the other cold gods.

Often enough, however, the old ways of understanding are absorbed and repurposed by the new story. Pagan figures of the Dutch and German yuletide merged with legends of an early Christian saint named Nicholas to form the modern idea of Santa Claus. The ritual of kissing beneath the mistletoe marks an old sexual metaphor absorbed into the Christmas tradition—as does the folksong "The Holly and the Ivy," which records the moment when the ancient imagery of green in the cold midwinter (the masculine holly for the men to praise in song, the feminine ivy for the women) was pulled into the Christian account of the season.

The question we have to face these days, however, is what happens when Christmas absorbs the conditions for its own meaning? When the huge, ungainly thing grows so big that it eats up even its Christianity? For Christmas has, over the past century, devoured Advent, gobbling it up with the turkey giblets and the goblets of seasonal ale. Yes, yes, I know: Every secularized holiday tends to lose, in public contexts, the meaning it holds in the religious calendar. Across the nation, even in some of the churches, Easter has hopped across Lent, Halloween has frightened away All Saints, and New Year's has swallowed up Epiphany.

Still, the disappearance of Advent in our common understanding is a difficulty—for it has injured even the secular Christmas season: opening a hole, from Thanksgiving on, that can be filled only with fiercer, madder, and wilder attempts to anticipate Christmas. More Christmas trees. More Christmas lights. More tinsel, more tassels, more glitter, more glee—until the glut of candies and carols, ornaments and trimmings, has left almost nothing for Christmas Day. For much of America—even for

me, out here in the Black Hills of South Dakota—
Christmas itself arrives as an afterthought: not the
fulfillment, but only the end, of the long yule season that has burned without stop since the stores
began their Christmas sales.

It's true that in the liturgical calendar, the season points ahead to Christmas. Advent genuinely
proclaims an *advent*—a *time before,* a *looking
forward*—and it lacks meaning without Christmas. But maybe Christmas, in turn, lacks meaning without the penitential season of Advent to go
before it. The daily Bible readings in the churches
during Advent are filled with visions of things
yet to be—a constant barrage of the future tense.
Think of Isaiah's *And it shall come to pass . . . And
there shall come forth . . .* A longing pervades the
Old Testament selections read in the weeks before
Christmas—an anxious, almost sorrowful litany
of hope only in what has not yet come. Zephaniah.
Judges. Malachi. Numbers. *I shall see him, but not
now: I shall behold him, but not nigh: There shall*

*come a star out of Jacob, and a scepter shall rise out
of Israel.*

At its root, Advent is a discipline: a way of form-
ing anticipation and channeling it toward its goal.
There's a flicker of rose on the third Sunday—
Gaudete!, the Latin of that day's Mass begins:
Rejoice!—but then it's back to the dark purple
that is the sign of the season in liturgical churches.
And what those somber vestments symbolize is the
atonement and promise of reform we make during Advent. Nothing we do can earn us the gift of
Christmas, any more than Lent wins us Easter.
But a season of contrition and sacrifice prepares us
to understand and feel something about just how
great the gift is when at last the day itself arrives.

More than any other holiday, Christmas seems
to need its setting in the church year, for without
it we have a diminishment of language, a diminishment of culture, and a diminishment of imagination. The Jesse trees and the Advent calendars,
St. Martin's Fast and St. Nicholas's Feast—the

childless crèches, the candle wreaths, the vigil of Christmas Eve: They give a shape to the anticipation of the season. They discipline the ideas and emotions that would otherwise shake themselves to pieces, like a flywheel wobbling wilder and wilder until it finally snaps off its axle.

Maybe that's what has happened to Christmas, in the days since Dickens bestrode the season. The ideas and the emotions have all broken free and smashed their way across the fields. From Longfellow's *I heard the bells on Christmas Day / Their old, familiar carols play* to Irving Berlin's *I'm dreaming of a white Christmas / Just like the ones I used to know,* there has been, for a long time now, something oddly backward looking about Christmas lyrics—some nostalgia that insists on substituting its melancholy for the somber contrition and sorrow of Advent. In the same way, childhood memoirs have become the dominant form of Christmas writing. Often beautiful—from Dylan Thomas's *A Child's Christmas in Wales* to Lillian Smith's *Memories of a Large Christmas*—those stories nonetheless deploy their golden-hued Christmassy emotions only toward the past: a kind of contrite feeling without the structure of Advent's contrition; all the regret and sense of absence cast back to what has been and never will be again.

Meanwhile, weirdly, the forward-looking parts of Advent have also escaped the discipline of the season. In certain ways, the season has become little except anticipation—anticipation run amuck, like children so sick with expectation that the reality can never be satisfying when it finally arrives. This, too, is something broken off from the liturgical year: another group of adventual feelings without the Advent that gave them form, another set of Christmas ideas set loose to drive themselves mad.

Back in the early 1890s, William Dean Howells published a funny little fable called "Christmas Every Day." Once upon a time, the story begins, "there was a little girl who liked Christmas so much that she wanted it to be Christmas every day in the year." What's more, she found a fairy to grant her wish, and she was delighted when Christmas came again on December 26, and December 27, and December 28.

Of course, "after it had gone on about three or four months, the little girl, whenever she came into the room in the morning and saw those great ugly, lumpy stockings dangling at the fireplace, and the disgusting presents around everywhere, used to sit down and burst out crying. In six months she was perfectly exhausted, she couldn't even cry anymore." By October, "people didn't carry presents around nicely anymore. They flung them over the fence or through the window, and, instead of taking great pains to write 'For dear Papa,' or 'Mama' or 'Brother,' or 'Sister,' they used to write, 'Take it, you horrid old thing!' and then go and bang it against the front door."

These days, by the time Christmas actually rolls around, it feels as though this is very nearly what we've had: Christmas every day, at least since

Thanksgiving. Often it starts even earlier. This year I started receiving the glossy catalogues of Christmas clothing and seasonal bric-a-brac in September, and there were Christmas-shopping ads on the highway billboards before Halloween. The anticipatory elements reach a crescendo by early December, and their constant scream makes the sudden quiet of Christmas Day almost a relief from the Christmas season.

I don't remember quite this much opposition, the battle between Christmas and the Christmas season, when I was young. When I was little (ah, the nostalgia of the childhood memoir), I always felt that the days right before Christmas were a time somehow out of time. Christmas Eve, especially, and the arrival of Christmas itself at midnight: the hours moved in ways different from their passage in ordinary time, and the sense of impending completion was like a flavor to the air I breathed.

I've noticed in recent years, however, that this

feeling comes over me more rarely than it used to, and for shorter bits of time. I have to pursue the sense of wonder, the taste in the air, and cling to it self-consciously. Even for me, the endless roar of untethered Christmas anticipation is close to drowning out the disciplined anticipation of Advent. And when Christmas itself arrives, it has begun to seem a day not all that different from any other. Oh, yes, church and home to a big dinner. Presents for the children. A set of decorations. But nothing special, really.

This is what Advent, rightly kept, would halt—the thing, in fact, Advent is designed to prevent. Through all the preparatory readings, through all the genealogical Jesse trees, the somber candles on the wreaths, the vigils, and the hymns, Advent keeps Christmas on Christmas Day: a fulfillment, a perfection and completion, of what had gone before. *I shall see him, but not now: I shall behold him, but not nigh.*

V

TINSEL. NO ONE needs tinsel. Even the word is a tinselly kind of word. It ought to have been a mild profanity, suitable for bridge clubs and 1950s sorority girls: "Oh, tinsel, I forgot my keys again, Suzie." Instead, it names one of the most destructive substances known to humankind. Originally cut from sheets of lead foil—till somebody finally noticed that it was turning children's livers purple and green—the loathsome stuff evolved through various tin and aluminum incarnations to become the plastic killer that it is today. Tinsel murdered my vacuum cleaner this Christmas. Sucked up into the air vents, the little ribbons wrapped themselves around the motor, melted, and smothered the helpless appliance. Tinsel smoked, and tinsel sparked, and tinsel set off the fire alarm. And now, on top of all the other holiday expenses, I have to drive to the store and buy a new vacuum cleaner.

I should probably pick up more wrapping paper while I'm out. There's never enough of the stuff. Has anyone else noticed something strange, something slightly disturbed, about wrapping paper? It's a neurosis, really: this desire to grab anything that isn't moving and swaddle it in oddly printed sheets of red and green. A genuine psychological disease; hebephrenia, maybe, but I can't be sure because all my reference books have been shoved back on their shelves to make room for the piles of tissue paper, rolls of bright ribbons, and endless tubes of wrapping paper.

My wife and daughter are both mad wrappers. They love the whole panoply of Christmas coverings. They box, bedeck, and bundle. They camouflage, cloak, and case. They drape, enfold, mask, muffle, pack, sheathe, shroud, and veil. I can see my daughter, happy as a bird, perched at the dining room table, hand-coloring paper to wrap the hand-painted box that holds the hand-made present she made for her great-grandmother. The tip of her tongue sneaks to the corner of her mouth in her concentration, and she hums with the carols she's put on the CD player to help her along.

It's cute as a button, I know, but I go through periods when I don't get it. I mean, nearly every purchased gift comes prepackaged from the manufacturer in plastic and brightly printed cardboard, or nestled in a nice little box, and usually shrink-wrapped as well. And as soon as we buy it, we immediately clothe it in yet more layers of extraneous material: cotton batting, and tissue paper, and wraps, and boxes, and containers. My daughter spent weeks working on her presents—and now weeks more working on their wrapping, abetted by her mother: "I know, honey! Let's pack your aunts' presents in tissue paper and put them inside these nice little bags with the string handles! That way you can paint Christmas designs on the bags, too!"

Oh, goody. The mailman just brought the annual package from friends in Wyoming. Why do we have to open it? We know what it is. There's the brown grocery bag paper, which covers the corrugated-cardboard box, which contains the Styrofoam peanuts, which bury the red and green wrapping paper, which surrounds the tin cookie box, which holds the sheets of wax paper, which envelop the homemade sugar cookies. The same homemade sugar cookies our friends send every year. All of which will be broken, because sugar cookies just don't travel well.

And don't get me started on those padded mailing envelopes filled with recycled lint. For years now, the insufferable things have been the package of choice for small breakables at Christmastime. Perhaps they work better than any alternative, but mostly they seem to exist to spray gray dust and clumps of dryer fluff across the living room carpet.

Ah, well. Christmas comes like a fire every year—a burning declaration of warmth and brightness in the December cold and dark. It's a stance, really, a theological choosing of sides:

against the rising chill of the fall, God gave us this burning flame of the Christ child, and with that impossible generosity, we will stand. Why should it be a surprise that such theology has consequences in our winter psyches? A preference for bright colors, a wish to decorate and adorn, a hunger for extravagance, a desire for celebration?

On Christmas Day, after church, I'll see the tree all gussied up, a bandits' den of brightly colored gifts underneath it. I'll watch my daughter open her presents—gently and carefully, not wanting to tear the pretty wrappings. I'll smell the Christmas dinner beginning in the kitchen and hear the old familiar anthems play. I'll look around in satisfaction at the wild mess of wrapping paper and opened packages and stray pine needles and scattered cookie crumbs. And I'll remember that I forgot to buy the new vacuum cleaner to clean it all up.

Oh . . . tinsel.

Chapter 4

O Little Town

We write these words now, many miles distant from the spot at which, year after year, we met on that day. . . . And yet the old house, the room, the merry voices and smiling faces, the jest, the laugh, the most minute and trivial circumstances connected with those happy meetings, crowd upon our mind at each recurrence of the season.

—*THE PICKWICK PAPERS*

I

LATE AFTERNOON ON Christmas Eve, the year I was eleven, my father took me with him across the river. I can't remember exactly what the hurry was, but he was a busy lawyer, and he needed some papers signed by a rancher who lived on the other side of the Missouri. So off we headed, west across the bridge from Pierre and north through the river hills.

If you've never seen that South Dakota country in winter, you have no idea how desolate land can be. I once asked my grandmother why her family had decided to stop their wagon trek in what became the prairie town where she was born. And she answered, in surprise I didn't know, "Because that's where the tree was." *The* tree. The empty hills were frozen dry, as my father and I drove along, with sharp ice crystals blowing up from the knots of cold, gray grass.

Now, we were supposed to stay for only a minute or two, get a signature, and turn back for home. But you can't pay a visit in South Dakota, especially at Christmastime, without facing food—endless besieging armies of it, and usually the worst of American holiday cuisine: Jell-O molds with carrot shavings, chocolate-packet pies, neon-pink hams pricked to death with cloves and drowned in honey.

If you've never seen one of those prairie tables, you have no idea how desolate food can be.

From the moment she spotted us turning off the highway, Mrs. Harmon must have been piling her table with hospitality. I remember eating cinnamon buns crusted with sugar while Mr. Harmon and his two tall sons told us about the coyote tracks they'd found that morning. It was the cold that made the coyotes risk it, scenting the trash cans, probably, and the livestock had been skittish all day. But then Mrs. Harmon began to shout, "Jim, Jim, the horses are out." And in a tangle of arms and jackets, we poured out to herd back the frightened animals.

By the time we were done, however, four expensive quarter-horses were loose on the prairie. Cursing, Mr. Harmon climbed into his pickup and headed north along the highway, while my father drove off to the south. Mrs. Harmon took it more calmly. She went inside to telephone the neighbors, and the boys began to saddle three horses to ride out and look.

You have to understand the significance of that third horse, for it marks the difference between town and country—even a small town surrounded by country, like Pierre. The Harmons simply assumed an eleven-year-old boy was old enough to help, while my mother would have pitched a fit at the idea of my riding out on the prairie, a few hours from sundown, in the middle of winter.

In fact, there was little chance of getting lost. I knew, more or less, how to ride, and the highway was in sight much of time. Still, as the land grew colder and darker, the excitement faded, leaving only brittle determination, a boy's will not to be the first to turn back.

I can't have ridden far through the Christmas hills—maybe three or four miles—when I came over a rise and spotted one of the horses, skittering in front of a worn farmhouse. Standing in the yard was a woman, a rope in one hand and her other hand held up empty toward the horse. She was hatless and tiny, hardly bigger than I was, with a man's heavy riding coat hanging down below her knees, the sleeves turned back to show the faded lining, and she seemed very old to me. Yellow light streamed out on the cold ground from the one lit window of the house.

As I rode down, she waved me back, talking to the horse in the gentlest, lightest patter, as though nothing much had ever been wrong, really, and, anyway, everything was all right now. He bobbed back and forth, nearer and nearer, until he touched her open hand with his steaming nose and she eased the loop over his neck.

"Bea Harmon called," she said, handing me the rope, "and told me you were all out looking for this boy. They often come to me, you know. He'll go along quietly now."

Her eyes were quick and black. "I don't see many people, here about," she chirruped, like a winter bird. "Come in and get warm. I'll make some coffee. No, you're a little young for coffee. I'll put some water on for tea, and there're the cookies I made in case someone came by." But I was proud of bringing back one of the strays and wouldn't wait. I shied away from her outstretched hand and galloped back.

Sometimes you catch sight of a turn, heading off into the distance—a dirt track or a county road at right angles to the highway, as you drive along those straight, miles-long lines you find only in the West. And you know you'll never go up it, never come back to find where it leads, and always there remains a sense, as you roll past, that maybe this time you should have turned and followed that track up into the distant hills.

Her hair was the same thin shade of gray as the weather-beaten pickets of the fence around her frozen garden. She had a way with horses, and she was alone on Christmas Eve. There is little in my life I regret as much as that I would not stay for just one cookie, just one cup of tea.

II

A CHILDREN'S TOY catalogue came in the mail the other day, or, rather, an adult's toy catalogue, filled with the opportunity for aging grown-ups to buy, at outrageous prices, the toys of their childhood. There were Sting Ray bicycles with banana seats and giant U-shaped handle bars trailing multicolored streamers from the plastic handgrips. There were Slinkies, pogo sticks, cap guns, and the kind of open-springed, bouncing nursery horses no liability-conscious manufacturer would dare offer children anymore.

All those toys I hungered for when I was young: Just hearing their names is like listening to an ancient, half-forgotten litany of secular Christmas. Tinker Toys, Erector Sets, and Lincoln Logs. Creepy Crawlers, Flexible Flyers, Raggedy Ann, and Raggedy Andy. They have the rhythm of plainchant, of hymns lifted up to Santa Claus. Silly Putty, Super Balls, and Matchbox cars. Duncan yo-yos, paint-by-number sets, and 3-D viewers. Aggravation, Stratego, Trouble, and Operation. Etch A Sketches and Spirographs. Model space-ships, antique cars, and Billy Bishop's World War I biplanes. A German Fokker triplane I snapped the wheels off while trying to glue on the third wing.

I can't remember now exactly why I so des-perately wanted Rock'em Sock'em Robots and A Barrel of Monkeys, Pivot Pool and Battleship, or anything made by Wham-O. Few of them came. We were not wealthy, and insofar as my parents held much of what passed for advanced ideas in those days, they believed in that vague kind of middle-American progressivism that expressed it-self in Scandinavian furniture, subscriptions to *The New Yorker,* and the purchase of "educational play-things." And of the few widely commercialized toys we did receive, none survive. Did they wear out? Were they victims of the brutal triage—the hurried abandoning of the incidental, the unnecessary, and the overlooked—that always happens just before the moving vans arrive? (Three moves is as good as a fire, my grandmother used to say—quoting Ben Franklin, I learned years later.) Or were they simply too disappointing to care much about once they came: cleaner, sharper, more memorable to desire than to obtain?

In a box at the back of my closet, a few last things remain: odds and ends sent on to me in adulthood by my mother, for the most part, as she came across them here and there in never-opened moving cartons tucked away in the basement or old shoe boxes hidden for years on the shelves behind the winter coats. I cannot impose order on it all. The recollections remain precise and perfect, in one sense, but they are only shards: exact bits of some mosaic whose overall pattern has faded; the broken pieces of a glass ornament, sharp enough to cut but no longer able to be reassembled.

I suppose that's why, when I think of the

Christmases of my childhood, I'm reduced to list making, as though, only by careful inventory, could I somehow call up again the feeling once invested, like a savings account, in the toys I had: A stuffed tiger, one eye askew, its neck ribbon shredding in age. (But where is the enormous bear my grandfather gave us when I was three, taller than either my sister or me?) A paperweight of Indian-head pennies mounted in clear plastic, a loose wheel off a model airplane, a small set of toy cars. A handful of mounted knights, the stones of their painted castle long since overgrown and tumbled down. A gold-braided military bandsman in a red tunic, the sole survivor of a regiment of plastic soldiers I once tried to march down the hall and across the living room of my grandparents' house in Rapid City during the middle of a party to raise money for Korczak Ziolkowski, the mad sculptor who was trying to carve an entire Black Hills mountain into a five-hundred-foot-tall statue of Crazy Horse. When the first high heels and the huge black wingtips of the lawyers and businessmen came smashing down on the soldiers, Korczak suddenly stooped down and gathered me up on his lap, his wild beard sweeping back and forth across my head while he laughed and drank, waving his arms and shouting at the guests to watch where they stepped until at last my grandmother took me up to bed.

But even the actual objects conjure up little more than the ghosts of how one remembers it must have felt at the time. Curiously, the memory is a little stronger, the image a little firmer, in recollecting the buying of presents, rather than the getting: the simultaneous feeling of titanic generosity and utter miserliness, a calculation of love measured to the penny, and an irrecoverable sensation—the proud knowledge that one has, in a fit of magnanimity, squandered every cent, matched with the shameful awareness of just how paltry the result is. If I spent the extra $1.43 to buy my older sister the metal stands instead of the plastic to hold her dolls, it was at the well-understood cost of buying the plastic tea set instead of the china for my younger sister. If I bought the Irish handkerchiefs for my grandfather, it was at the heartbreaking expense of the potholders for my mother. I've rarely judged anything as narrowly, and yet, even now, I'm not convinced that I shouldn't have gone with the taffy for my aunt and saved the money the chocolates cost to buy for my grandmother the larger size of glass ornament.

When I was eight, I decided that what my nine-year-old sister needed was the savings bank I found on the discount counter of a junk store, a coconut shell carved in the shape of a beatnik monkey, complete with beret, sunglasses, and bongo drums. But then, five blocks from home, Scooter's mother pulled over to offer me a ride. And it was while I was struggling to hold my packages, thank her, and climb inside that I knocked the monkey against the car door and cracked it down the middle. The grief was so sudden and precise, the desire not to let Scooter's mom see me cry so strong, the look on my face, reflected in the window of her Buick, so perfectly preserved in memory, that I can almost relive that sorrow just by remembering it.

And the next year as well, I was almost in tears as I walked home, listening to the dry snow squeak beneath the black rubber overshoes my mother made us wear, and with nothing but a Christmas card to give her after the store where I'd planned to get her genuine rhinestone earrings closed earlier than I had expected on Christmas Eve. But while I was trudging past the almost-deserted Christmas tree store in the Catholic school parking lot, a salesman suddenly leaned over the fence to ask if I wanted a wreath to take home. "I don't have enough money left," I said. "That's okay, kid," he answered. "We're closing up here. Give it to your mother. Tomorrow's Christmas."

III

IT WAS ALL too much. Long before Christmas it-self arrived, the season had taken us by the throats and shaken us into jelly. Who could stand against it? For that matter, who could stand it? The Advent calendars, the shopping, the candles, the bells. The cold wind that dried the snow to tiny balls of ice and piled them in crusted drifts against the walls of the breezeway. The snips of wrapping paper tracked from room to room. The fallen bits of tinsel trailed along the carpet. The carols that began their cease-less tintinnabulation the day after Thanksgiving and played until most of our capacity for emotion had been leached away.

By the end of the season, the carol-soundtracked Christmas rush had frazzled us into mad and mani-acal elves. I remember my little sister nearly slicing off her ear in the hurry to finish up on Christmas Eve as she tried to curl a ribbon by running it across a scissors' blade, the way she had seen the lady at the Montgomery Ward gift counter do. I remember my older sister snarling as she held together the ends of a package, waiting for the Elmer's glue to dry because the Scotch tape had run out.

Early in December, we were strong enough to take almost any amount of sentimentality in the stories our parents read to us nightly: Henry van Dyke's *The Other Wise Man*, Kate Douglas Wiggin's *Romance of a Christmas Card*, even my father's rendition of Washington Irving's *Old Christmas*. By the last week of Advent, the mere word Christmas could send us howling from the room.

Many of those nightly Christmas readings from my parents were *St. Nicholas* stories. Begun in 1873 and continuing until 1939, the monthly *St. Nicholas Magazine for Boys and Girls* was a dominant American publication in my grandparents' and great-grandparents' time. Under the editorship of Mary Mapes Dodge (a woman remembered these days, if remembered at all, only for her own children's book about a little Dutch boy named Hans Brinker and his attempt to win a pair of silver ice skates), the magazine printed the first works of everyone from Jack London to Eudora Welty. Stephen Vincent Benét, Ring Lardner, and Edna St. Vincent Millay all appeared as child writers in its pages, and its adult authors included Bret Harte, Theodore Roosevelt, and Laura Ingalls Wilder.

What *St. Nicholas* magazine wanted, more than anything else, was to instill the nation's moral vocabulary in the young. In the first issue's statement of editorial principles, Dodge demanded that the magazine's writers aim "to give clean, genuine fun to children of all ages. To give them examples of the finest types of boyhood and girlhood. . . . To foster a love of country, home, nature, truth, beauty, and sincerity. To prepare boys and girls for life as it is," and "to stimulate their ambitions—but along normally progressive lines."

Noble goals, no doubt, and we loved my mother's

battered 1960s reprint of *The St. Nicholas Anthology,* a book-length collection chosen by Henry Steele Commager (another now-faded name that signaled, once upon a time, just how established an institution the magazine had been). But many of those *St. Nicholas* stories proved that for sheer, unadulterated pap, you just can't beat the good, old-fashioned "normally progressive" lines.

There was, for instance, an 1885 story by Sophie Swett, called "How Santa Claus Found the Poor-House," about an orphan boy who didn't give up easily. "You might have known that he wouldn't give up easily," Swett points out, "by one glance at his sturdy little figure, at his bright, wide-open eyes, his firm mouth, and his square, prominent chin; even the little, turned-up end of his nose looked resolute." When I was eight or nine, the failure of my little figure to look sufficiently sturdy and resolute caused some comment from my older sister when we were sent out to shovel the driveway—to which I usually responded by mentioning her own deficiencies in the little-upturned-nose department, and we would end up rolling on the ground, trying to stuff snow down each other's back. I doubt, somehow, that's quite what the *St. Nicholas* crew had in mind.

I love Christmas stories, and yet, if you stop to think about it, isn't there something odd about the giving of Christmas books as Christmas presents? *The Christmas Almanac* and *The Little Big Book of Christmas. Uncle John's Bathroom Reader Christmas Collection* and *The Kingfisher Book of Classic Christmas Stories. The Collected Christmas Stories of Charles Dickens,* for that matter: I've never quite understood why people wrap them up as Christmas gifts. I mean, by the time you've actually gotten the book—and gone to church, and drunk the eggnog, and eaten the dinner, and cleaned up the wrapping paper, and squabbled with your sister, and blown out the candle stubs—Christmas is done for the year. All those endless seasonal volumes piled like a Mayan step pyramid down at the local bookstore: they exist primarily to gin up the Christmas spirits of their givers, rather than their receivers.

Of course, since gift-givers tend to be the actual purchasers of Christmas presents, it makes financial sense for publishers to concentrate on what inspires the buyers, rather than on what the incidental gift-getter might want to read. Which is probably why my keyword search at Amazon.com last year came up with 22,080 Christmas books in print—1,271 of them with the word *Christmas* in the title. From *An Affair Before Christmas* (a bodice-ripper in which the devilishly attractive Duke of Fletcher is determined to win back his beguiling bride's delectable affections) to *Shall I Knit You a Hat?* (a children's yarn in which Mother Rabbit knits Little Rabbit a Christmas hat to show off his long, beautiful ears), there's something for even the most jaded giver.

What the victims of these gifts think is another matter. I know it's only once a year, but that still seems a poor excuse for clogging up the bookshelves of your friends and relatives every twenty-fifth of December. Look, there are plenty of great stories out there for putting you in the Christmas mood. If it's a little yule comedy you want, try Max Beerbohm's parodies in *A Christmas Garland*. I've always had a soft spot for O. Henry's perfectly constructed tearjerker "The Gift of the Magi." Damon Runyon's "The Three Wise Guys" will never let you down—to say nothing of the second chapter of the Gospel of Luke.

But the time for reading all these comes in the days before Christmas, the fast run of Advent. Once Christmas itself has rolled around, it's gotten a little late for visions of sugarplums to dance in our heads. The true quiet time, the not-a-creature-stirring moment, isn't the night before Christmas. It comes the next evening, the night of Christmas itself, when finally everything calms down and there's room to look at all the books—from the aunts and uncles, the grandparents, the cousins, the family friends—that used to blizzard our Christmases when my sisters and I were young.

I'd build a bulwark on the bed after dinner and, book by book, browse them all. Zane Gray and Lord Dunsany. H. G. Wells and Arthur Conan Doyle. Dickens, always Dickens. Robert Louis Stevenson. The actual Christmas books—I remember *The Golden Book of Christmas Tales* in there somewhere—always came from our nonbookish friends and were politely but firmly set aside on Christmas night. That was the time for *R Is for Rocket,* and *Mr. Midshipman Hornblower,* and *Kim,* and *The Kid Who Batted 1.000.* I remember the slick feel of the purple dust jacket on *Journey to the Center of the Earth,* already on that first Christmas reading sliding off the book. I remember tearing through *Cannery Row* and *The Catcher in the Rye* because the paperbacks had such vivid covers I figured they had to be as good as *Shane* and *Podkayne of Mars.*

Those books had almost a taste, hard as it is

now to remember, and it came, I think, mostly from that irreproducible new-book smell: like slippery elm, maybe, or vanilla; a pulpy, wood-bark scent, compounded with linen and glue and black ink gall into a kind of oddly aged freshness, old and new at the same time. There was *The Lord of the Rings* when I was ten or eleven: three fat paperbacks packed in an illustrated cardboard case so tight that it ripped the first time I took them out. And there was *Homer Price* when I was six: an oversized, illustrated hardback, like a toddler's first steps out of picture books. *Freddy the Pig* and *The Wind in the Willows* and *Ivanhoe* and *A Canticle for Leibowitz* and on and on. They always seemed to smell like an impossible abundance in the midst of a cold winter.

But isn't that something like a metaphor for Christmas? The real Christmas, I mean: God's impossible abundance in the midst of a cold winter.

IV

BACK IN THE days I'd taken my wife and daughter to live in New York, we'd see him in December—the man at the sidewalk table selling *The Man with the Golden Arm*. Blowing on his hands, his steaming breath rising in the winter sun that slanted through Union Square, he offered for Christmas shoppers almost-pristine copies of books like *Ship of Fools* and *The Spy Who Came in from the Cold*.

To say nothing of *Games People Play*, Eric Berne's old pop-psychology best seller, and *Kon-Tiki*, Thor Heyerdahl's even older account of adventure on an ocean raft. Sloan Wilson's *The Man in the Gray Flannel Suit*, Dag Hammarskjöld's *Markings*, Barbara Tuchman's *A Distant Mirror*—perhaps a hundred used books, all of them carefully sealed in clear plastic envelopes as though they were rare and valuable volumes. As though they were classic editions. As though they were important.

From Here to Eternity and *Peyton Place, In Cold Blood* and *The Making of the President 1960, Sophie's Choice* and *The Peter Principle*—the funny thing is that I'd seen nearly all of them at my grandparents' house, one time or another. You know these books, too. Ernest Hemingway's *The Old Man and the Sea,* Patrick Dennis's *Auntie Mame,* Boris Pasternak's *Doctor Zhivago.* They were the permanent additions to the show-off shelves the middle class used to keep in their houses: the books that announced they were serious people.

Not too many books, you understand. Bohemians and college professors, beatniks and long-hairs, might live surrounded by text—everything from Lawrence Ferlinghetti's poetry in *A Coney Island of the Mind* to Ernst Cassirer's reinterpretation of intellectual history in *The Individual and the Cosmos in Renaissance Philosophy* (both of which I read one desperately snowbound winter break while house-sitting for a teacher in Georgetown).

You've seen those places; a friend describes them as "graduate student housing for grown-ups." The successful middle class of doctors and lawyers and bankers and such would never have allowed their beautiful homes to be overtaken by such clutter. But some books—many books, really, by today's standards—they did have to own. And to read.

The literary distinctions of those days were delicate. Such best sellers as James Michener's *Hawaii* and Harold Robbins's *The Carpetbaggers* were out of bounds, but such nearly equal best sellers as Moss Hart's *Act One* and William L. Shirer's *The Rise and Fall of the Third Reich* were required. Yes, to Saul Bellow's *Herzog*. No, to Ian Fleming's *You Only Live Twice*. And maybe, to Louis Nizer's *My Life in Court*. I could see them all again, in memory, while I browsed the bookseller's table on that New York sidewalk. The dust jacket on my grandparents' copy of *The Caine Mutiny* was blue, with silly drawings of naval officers. *The Confessions of*

Nat Turner was orange, with a newspaper typeface, like an old-fashioned broadside. *Myra Breckinridge* I can't remember. My grandmother wouldn't let me read it.

Franny and Zooey, Travels with Charley, Rabbit Redux: These best sellers didn't count as intellectual books, exactly, and they certainly weren't academic studies. What they were, really, were the highbrow end of the selections offered by the middlebrow Book of the Month Club. I checked, and, sure enough, most of the plastic-wrapped books on the cold Christmas table had the little indentation on the back cover that marked them as book club editions—which made them even less valuable to collectors.

Besides, all of the titles were genuine best sellers: thousands and thousands of copies in the first print run. *Rare* and *collectible* were not applicable words, but I wanted them. I wanted them all. The display of such books on those white floor-to-ceiling shelves built through the public spaces of the house—the living room, the parlor, that drinking room they called the library: This was how an entire class of people like my grandparents told the world that they were prosperous, cultured people. Able to hold an intelligent conversation without making a show of intellectualism; capable of artistic appreciation without being artists.

Serious people, in other words. People of weight who nonetheless hadn't toppled over into eccentricity. The mainstay of American culture. That book table in Union Square was like the altar of a cargo cult. Browsing through the old titles, I found myself yearning to call back the vanished time. To build such white shelves and to place upon them such agreed-upon books. To set along the edges the tasteful sprigs of holly and the little Christmas crèches and decorations. To be a person of weight and balance and confidence.

It's curious to look back now and realize how much books defined my life when I was young. Not just my own books—all those volumes my sisters and I would order from the Scholastic Book Club catalogue or receive in the flurry of Christmas presents—but the books of my parents and grandparents: Rachel L. Carson's *The Sea Around Us* and John Gunther's *Inside Russia Today.* John Steinbeck's *The Winter of Our Discontent* and Jean Kerr's *Please Don't Eat the Daisies.* Edwin O'Connor's *The Last Hurrah,* for that matter. All gone, from shelves now gone as well.

V

MY FATHER ALWAYS insisted on an early Christmas breakfast, a huge feast of eggs poached in milk, and bacon and hash browns and pancakes and marmalade and grapefruit and a sort of sweetened toast whose name I can't remember, but it tasted like corrugated cardboard with cinnamon and sugar sprinkled on top.

And then, after that groaning meal, nothing.

No lunch, no snack, no Christmas gingerbread, no nuts, no fruit. None of the fancy chocolate a cousin sent every year from San Francisco, none of the *bûche de Noël* my college-age sister taught us to make when she came back from her junior year in France with her bangs cut at a Parisian angle and her diary filled with recipes. Nothing until three o'clock, or four, or five, or, one year, even six, when the ravenous aunts had begun to snip at each other in hunger, and the starved uncles were snarling in the living room about how many terms Sigurd Anderson had been governor, and the children—past the wheedling stage, past the whining stage, past the stage of sitting on the kitchen floor and weeping for food—were crouched together on the sofa, dumb with misery.

But then at last the kitchen door would swing open in a blast of steam and smoke and relief. And the dining room table would fill with a turkey or a goose, rolls and salad and green beans, little glass bowls of watermelon pickles with tiny three-pronged forks beside them, and cranberries plopped whole in sugared water, boiled until they started to burst, then set aside to cool. "You see," my father explained every year as we sat down to eat, "this is the way to do it: a big breakfast to stretch your stomach, then no lunch, so by dinnertime you're really ready for a full Christmas meal."

They can't actually have all been there the same year, but my memory puts together on the table sweet potatoes and yams, butternut squash and the white potatoes mashed with milk and butter that—in one of those family traditions by which chores get divvied up—we were told only Uncle Hugo could make well. But there was always the onion-and-breadcrumb dressing into which my father dumped two, three, four white tins of dried sage, sneaking back into the kitchen to add more when he thought no one was looking.

And then there were pies: made from pieces of cooked pumpkin kept in the freezer since October, apples up from the cellar, Mason jars of mincemeat.

The food was more enormous than it was complicated. The only elaborate thing I remember my mother making for Christmas was an aspic, a sort of clarified gelatin made from a consommé of veal bones and flavored with tomatoes. I have no idea where she got the idea—South Dakota didn't run much to that sort of cooking—but she would spend hours working on it.

I can't describe how much we hated that aspic. It looked like horror-movie gore, and it tasted like Jell-O made with tomato juice. The relatives would ooh and aah as it was brought triumphantly on a platter to the table, and the crisis of the children's refusal to eat it would escalate from parental glares to harsh whispers to my father banging the table and forbidding us to have dessert until we finished our portions. At last, while our parents snuck out to the porch to recover their nerves, our favorite uncle would pick up our untouched plates along with his own and head off to the kitchen, whistling. He couldn't stand the stuff either.

After dinner, there was champagne for the adults, and eggnog and cake, if anyone had room left for anything, and wood to add to the flames in the fireplace, and the annual adventure of fumbling in the basement with a flashlight when a bad bulb on the tree flared out and blew the fuse. There were giant Springbok jigsaw puzzles, and a round of bridge if my grandmother insisted, or one of the new board games to play with the visiting cousins. When I was very young, there were uncles to beg into lighting, one more time, the candles on the miraculous little machine that caught the rising heat of the flames to spin a fan that whirled around small brass angels with long wands, ringing miniature bells with each revolution. And then there were books, and more books, and yet more books—until everything we had wanted Christmas to be seemed present in the dead of those cold winters.

VI

AND YET, FULFILLMENT always comes with disappointments of its own. By the end of Christmas Day, we were satisfied—and sated: drained of wonder and prone to a reaction against the overindulgence, the replete, in a season of charity. This was in the years before the nation had completely surrendered to its secular, store-bought fate, the era in which every newspaper in America ran an editorial sometime during the season bemoaning the commercialization of Christmas. Ours was a sterner, more puritanical objection, however. We did not lack the religious meaning of Christmas; we had churchgoings and Bible readings, candles and Advent calendars, angels on the tree and carols insisting Christ was born *that man no more may die.* But we had something else as well, something that turned us away with an odd distaste from the explosion of opened presents, ribbons spread across the floor, and bright balls of crumpled wrapping paper, red and green—the living room transformed into Ali Baba's cave or Hollywood's vision of a bandits' lair.

I remember bundling up and going out for air after Christmas dinner the year I was sixteen. Trudging along the lip of the white-dusted gully on the edge of the western plains, I looked out to see the land, like a cold sea stretching off to the horizon. Cities on an ocean shoreline have a choice: they can turn their faces to the sea, or turn their backs—lining the shore with pretty hotels and rich homes or edging the water with dim warehouses, narrow streets, and greasy piers. But all prairie towns turn their backs to the prairie. They have to. The huddled houses form a storm-battened island in the midst of endless space.

But sometimes in winter I could sense something else in that cold, blank range—or, rather, *nothing* else, emptiness itself like a positive force, an overwhelmingly present absence: purer than we were, cleaner, truer to God's purposes, more real.

Once, years later, I felt it again. It was near midnight, while I was driving across the state to Pierre
in an old rust-orange Ford pickup. Expecting to
see the lights of the car that had followed me from
Brookings to Huron, I glanced into the rearview
mirror and saw . . . nothing—the absolute nothing, a darkness from before creation. It was like
falling into deep water at night, and before I awoke,
I was off the highway, the gravel clattering in the
wheel wells and the weeds snapping off as they tore
against the fenders.

The prairie in December is brutal and indifferent, but that sated Christmas I was sixteen—with
presents back home spilling off the sofa, the annual
racecar track looped in a figure eight beneath the
tree, too many new books and boxes of candy, the
mothball odor of the Christmas linen and the cloying scent of the evergreen branches—I perceived,
in some confused adolescent's way, the spirit's har-
rowing side. *I came to cast fire upon the earth,* as

Christ declares in the Gospel of Luke, *and would that it were already kindled!* There was a burned-over purity to that frozen South Dakota landscape, an icy clarity to its ash-white slate. There was an escape from the mess and clutter of our overpopulated Christmas desires, ruined by their secular attainment. To stand along the prairie's rim was to understand the clean, impatient thought of hermits and the Desert Fathers: where human beings are, the divine is not. God lives apart from people.

Of course, at other times, I have sensed, on the edge of perception, a little of the counter-thought: a portion of the opposite truth about God and people. In most of my recollections of the Dakota prairies, the wind is blowing. Sheltered down between the river hills—picking chokecherries with my grandmother in the hollows by the cemetery or playing with my friends in the gullies left by the flash floods—I felt it less. But out on the giants' dancing plain, the wind seemed never to stop. Sometimes in the fall, the family would go rock collecting on the buttes northeast of Pierre. And I always wondered why my parents didn't seem to hear how much the wind was filled with anger, stunting the trees and twisting the scrub—gouging at anything that stood upright, scaling our skin and eyes, screeching in our ears cruelties and obscenities just beyond the edge of understanding. I would come home sick and trembling at the promises the wind had made.

Once, back on January 12, 1888, the wind made good on its promise, and a hundred children died. Hundreds of adults, as well, and thousands of horses and cows. First came the blasts of frigid air, followed quickly by the haze of ice dust that sliced the skin from the farmers caught outside. Then came the snow, and then the killing cold. The late morning had been mild, rising into the 30s around noon, but the temperature soon started dropping rapidly: losing, at one measuring station, 18 degrees in four minutes. By midnight it was 40 below—70 degrees lost in half a day.

The writer David Laskin once set himself to study the storm by reading the surviving journals of the Norwegian and German immigrants who rushed to fill the Dakota plains in the early 1880s. In the resulting book, *The Children's Blizzard*, Laskin tells story after story of that grim day: Some of the children trapped at school tried to make it home. A few survived, burrowing into haystacks or forming rings in which the outer children froze to death keeping the littlest children alive inside their hug. Many others, however, were lost. Townsmen were blown out to the prairie as they tried to cross the street. Farmers were between their houses and their barns. "William Klemp, a newly married Dakotan in the full vigor of young manhood," Laskin writes, "left his pregnant wife and went out in the storm to care for their livestock. He never returned. . . . It was spring when they found his body in a sod shanty a mile from the house."

The Great Blizzard of 1888 changed little on

the Great Plains; the cold, indifferent prairie had seen bad storms before and would see them again. Something did change, however, in that winter blast. Never again would the rest of America—or the Dakotans themselves, for that matter—see the prairie as ready land, open for settlement. By 1900, only twelve years later, 60 percent of the inhabitants had fled back east or on to California. A frenzy about the "schoolchildren's blizzard" seized America's newspapers, which did have the good result of leading Congress to create what would become the National Weather Service. The major effect of all that publicity, however, was a general conclusion that the western prairie was unlivable, and the decline of population on the old buffalo commons continued for decades. People will stay in places where the temperature gets to 105 in the summer. And they will settle even where the temperature gets to 40 below in the winter. But they won't stay long in places where it does both.

Lord knows, those nineteenth-century settlers

tried: believing that if only they worked hard enough, and prayed hard enough, they could compel the land to support them. To visit that bleak South Dakota prairie now—coming upon the little towns with their water towers, their white houses, and their cemeteries filled with upright headstones—is to recognize the price the homesteaders paid, for each of those towns was carved from the plains, grave by grave. Inside are carefully planted trees and tended hedges, small parks, right-angled corners with stop signs and streets laid out square on the compass: an aiming at an ordered life.

Outside lies the wilderness—not the manicured wilderness of postcard-pretty rain forests and the picturesque mountain peaks beloved by the designers of national parks, but the real thing. A cold that kills. Pestilence and blight. Plagues of locusts and blackbirds and dust. A summer sun that dries up the streambeds and bakes the high-banked cattle reservoirs into cracked-earth packets before they fall to dust and blow away.

This is no countryside for hermits or loners or those who think they don't need company. In one important way, the harsh prairies remain today exactly what they were in 1888: a world in which people must help one another to build their barns and raise their livestock, to educate their children, to worship in their churches. And sometimes, out on those Christmas plains, that truth is visible. I recognize it when I think of the lost horse and the woman at the old gray farmhouse in the river hills when I was eleven. I see it when I remember heading back home from my walk to sit with my sisters and look at our books, the Christmas I was sixteen. I catch a glimpse of it even now, setting presents for my own daughter beneath the tree.

And why shouldn't we be able to perceive that truth of companionship? It was signaled for us long ago, by a child laid in swaddling clothes within a manger. God works through people: where human beings are, there the divine has chosen to be.

Chapter 5

As I Wander

Time was, with most of us, when Christmas Day
encircling all our limited world like a magic ring,
left nothing out for us to miss or seek; bound together all our home enjoyments, affections, and
hopes; grouped everything and everyone around the
Christmas fire.

*—WHAT CHRISTMAS IS
AS WE GROW OLDER*

I

I REMEMBER THE woman screaming on Park
Avenue, a few days before Christmas, one of those
winters we spent in New York. "It's not my fault,"
she raged into her cell phone, flecks of saliva on
the corners of her mouth. Over and over, like the

high-pitched whine of a power saw cutting bricks: *It's not my fault, you —ing —. It's not my fault, you evil —. It's . . . not . . . my . . . fault.*

I don't know, maybe it really wasn't her fault, whatever *it* was. But her cell phone and makeup, her dark purse and blue coat, her warm leather gloves— the accoutrements of sanity around that face of public madness—made her seem guilty. Guilty of something, down to the bone. The man at the Salvation Army kettle kept his tense back turned against her as he rang his Christmas bell. The crowds of passing strangers fixed their eyes at uncomfortable angles and hurried by. I saw the screaming woman for a moment framed by the giant candy canes and white Christmas garlands soaped on the window of the storefront behind her. Then the traffic light changed, and I crossed the street, my shoulders hunched in self-protection. *It's not my fault, you evil —. It's . . . not . . . my . . . fault.*

Is twice a warning or only a coincidence? For I heard the phrase a second time that day, in the vestibule of the bank after work. New York is still one of the world's great Christmas cities. Too dirty for too long to clean up well just for the holidays, Manhattan still makes a brave show for the season. The shop-window mannequins sport their Christmas finery, and the railings on the apartment buildings don their strings of lights and tinsel. Maybe movies—from *Miracle on 34th Street* on down—are what have made New York's Christmases seem so iconic: the ice skating at Rockefeller Center, the skimpy elf costumes on the strutting Rockettes across at Radio City, the sleigh bells on the horse cabs, the piles of toys at F.A.O. Schwarz, the windows at Lord & Taylor. But at least, as a result, New York still tries. There in the bank, while I waited in line for an automatic teller machine, I watched the city's shoppers hurrying past, their arms full of Christmas packages, and listened to a man talking loudly on his cell phone, one foot up on the windowsill.

"It's not my fault," he explained in a confident

boom. "I'm just the kind of person who has to keep after things." What is it about self-justification that always makes it seem so false? About that phrase "I'm just the kind of person who" that makes it sound like the beginning of a lie? He was well dressed in loafers and slacks, a nice overcoat, and apparently indifferent to the fact that the people at the ATMs could overhear him. With the effortless patter of a story told many times before—with the sort of smooth charm, in fact, that fails because it announces too openly how charming it is trying to be—he launched into a complicated story about how he didn't really want to sue anyone, but then he was the kind of person who needed to see that he got his rights, and it wasn't his fault everything got so messed up.

It's not my fault—the cry we've made every day since Adam took the apple. Down somewhere in the belly, there's an awareness of just how wrong this world is, how fallen and broken and incomplete. This is the guilty knowledge, the failure of innocence, against which we snarl and rage: that's just the way the world is; there's nothing I can do; I didn't start things; it's not my fault. What would genuine innocence look like, if it ever came into the world? I know the answer my faith calls me to believe: like a child born in a cattle shed. But to understand why that is an answer, to see it clearly, we are also compelled to know our guilt for the world, to feel it all the way to the bottom.

I sometimes wonder to whom all the city's cell phone talkers are talking. People all around them, thousands and thousands: *there*, that angry balding man slamming past in a stained parka, and *there*, that coatless woman with the deliberately unfocused stare smokers wear as they stand with their arms crossed outside restaurants, and *there*, that tired-looking girl in the sweater trying to stop a taxi, and *there*, and *there*, and *there*—an endless stream of presence, and still they shout or murmur on the street, pouring secrets and imprecations into their clenched phones and headsets. Speaking to the ones who aren't there, communing with the absent like fortune-tellers peering into a crystal ball. Like mediums calling the dead.

Sometimes New York hints at something different. There's a strange impression the city gives after a snowstorm—a kind of epiphanic feeling, a sense of being taken for a moment out of time. People walk down the middle of the streets. A few pull out their skis and slalom along First Avenue. The taxis all disappear, and for an instant the whitewashed city looks clean and small-townish.

But New York cannot play for long at being the New Jerusalem. The ultimate time-bound place, it cannot step outside the rush and rattle of commerce. The supreme City of Man, it cannot pose as the City of God. With their town whitewashed and almost pretty, New Yorkers act for a few moments as though things have changed—or rather, as though these few moments don't count, as though the storm had lifted them out of normal life and the overlay of snow had reformed them into the untainted and unhurried. I remember seeing an old-fashioned toboggan –ten or twelve feet long, the wooden slats curling to a two-foot swoosh in front—being drawn along Fourteenth Street, filled with laughing children. Who has room to store a toboggan in Manhattan, on the off chance of snow? Someone, clearly. Someone who has been waiting years for the white apocalypse.

But most Christmases, there are only cold drizzles, the icy rain that that never washes anything clean. I emptied my pockets on the way home from the bank: another Salvation Army kettle, a drunk man on the sidewalk with a hand-lettered sign I couldn't read, a woman rattling change in a paper cup. I sometimes hate the city, all tarted up in its tawdry Christmas clothes. Mewing us together on its streets, it forces us to see the human stain. It forces us to know. *It's not my fault,* I muttered as I blew on my cold hands. May God have mercy on us all. *It's . . . not . . . my . . . fault.*

II

ALL THE YEARS I lived and worked back east, my grandmother would plead with me to settle back in Pierre. Not that it did much good, for I always felt I had put in my time on the prairies. I had paid my dues on those hard plains as a child, and besides, even when my sisters and I were children, the cool shadow of the Black Hills looked to us like the proper summer place: The crumbling rock, speckled with mica. The dark trees. The cold creeks. The small trestles on which we'd climb, marking where the failed railroad of the gold miners had once tried to drive a straight line through the twisting hills. If, in adulthood, New York came to seem a winter town, then the Black Hills were still marked by summer: a park to which I could retreat with my wife and daughter, away from the East.

Maybe that's why Lorena and I bought the used Jaguar convertible, once we had found the rambling mess of the Victorian summer house in

Hot Springs. We needed something to get around in (like many New Yorkers, we didn't drive, much less own a car, in the city). And if the little roadster was wildly impractical in a place where half the roads are dirt or gravel tracks, it was also a lot of fun to take out on the two-lane blacktops that wind through the weathered granite spires, like needles of gray rock, in the central Black Hills.

Besides, the car was cheap. Or cheap, anyway, to buy. Actually owning the thing turned out to be a more expensive proposition. Your typical British sports car needs roughly one hour of mechanical work for every hour on the road, and that old Jaguar seemed determined to uphold all the fine old British traditions. A twelve-cylinder motor! Jet-black paint! Leather seats! Fan belts and tubing apparently modeled after the confusion of a London street map! An oil leak determined to keep Saudi Arabia in business for generations to come!

But it was a summer car—and how much

reliability does anyone need from such things? I remember we parked it one day, toward the middle of June, across the street from the town's ice-cream parlor, in one of the diagonal parking spaces overlooking the river. Fall River, it's called, although the word *river* is maybe a little much. It's really more of an overachieving creek, formed by the dozens of hot springs in the area. For that matter, *hot* is a little much. The Truth-in-Naming Commission would have demanded the town be called Lukewarm Springs instead. Water bubbling from the ground around 60 degrees may keep the river from freezing over the winter, but we had come to South Dakota for the summer, and along about July, those springs feel a long way north of hot. Or even warm.

Still, Hot Springs is a pretty place, nestled in the last mountain canyon before the evergreens of the Black Hills give over to the treeless prairies to the south. Through much of the West, the softwoods are what reveal the presence of water: cottonwoods, maybe an elm or two, some poplars, an occasional oak. And Hot Springs has something of that prairie town feel—backed, however, by the mountains of ponderosa pine and Black Hills spruce. All in all, a perfect place to spend our summers, we thought: a small-town, semirural escape from the pressures of New York and Washington, with Internet access and a fun convertible for cruising around, whenever it decided to run.

Which is why the Jaguar was parked across from the ice-cream parlor when the flatbed truck, loaded with a gigantic piece of farm machinery, came slowly around the curve. The ice-cream cones were pretty good. My daughter chose the maple nut, I think. My wife picked the huckleberry. And the mower arm on the harvester decided to break loose and scoop up the row of cars parked across the street.

It was a slow-motion catastrophe, the whole thing happening at a leisurely twenty miles an hour. *Bam,* and the bed of the Ford pickup was smashed. Then the mower arm calmly recoiled back to the truck that was carrying it, bounced against the tractor, and swung out again—just in time to crush the old station wagon parked in the second spot. *Bam,* swing back, swing out again, and *bam,* hit the next car. And the next was our little black Jaguar, with the top closed, waiting its turn.

Bad wiring may be the most famous feature of vintage British sports cars. (An old car-enthusiasts' joke runs: Why do the English drink warm beer? Because the same company that makes the electrical systems for their automobiles also makes their refrigerators.) But those little cars are equally notable for how low they are to the ground. These aren't vehicles you step down from. They're cockpits you climb up out of, and when the mower arm reached the Jaguar, it almost passed right over it. Almost. Just the lowest tine of the mower caught the car, slicing as delicately as a surgeon's scalpel through the cloth roof, making a sort of convertible of the convertible—a roll-your-own sunroof added to the retractable top.

The smashup made the front page of the small town's newspaper the next week. And the man from the insurance company spent several helpful weeks hunting down an upholstery shop to sew a new roof for the poor torn car. But it was the local policeman, come to write up an accident report, who brought the matter home. "Summer folks, eh?" he asked. "Well, things like this happen, from time to time, out here. And up on the highway, it would have been worse. You might think about getting a different car. Something a little more solid, a little more South Dakota, if you know what I mean."

Summer folks? *Summer folks?* I was born in this state, I wanted to say, and I've worked its ranches, and hauled its hay, and ridden its horses. But I looked down at the pretty little scalped sports car, shining there in the sun, and I had to admit that I did know, pretty much, what he meant. A pickup or a jeep, maybe, would be more practical: something with a little higher clearance for the dirt roads and a little more protection for the passengers. But

I didn't think we would bother. We wanted a toy, for those warm summer days, as we drove through the playground that we imagined the Black Hills to be.

And yet, playgrounds—places defined by summer—are incomplete, in important ways, mostly because they're not real. Not entirely: not shaped by the responsibility that adults are supposed to take in this world. I remember, another June in South Dakota, watching a man drifting, dozing on an inner tube on the summer water a mile or so north of our house, and he didn't wake till he nudged the wall of scree and shattered rocks at the far end of the reservoir. The current is weak in that little Cold Brook lake, formed by piling earth and broken boulders across the neck of a red-rock canyon. But there was enough to coast him slowly, peacefully, inexorably down the hundred yards to the stone-littered hill of the dam—where he woke with a yelp and a startled leap at the touch of the sharp-edged stones.

I remember a woman, too, drifting on the shore:

a floppy straw hat, a green-print towel draped over her legs, and the black leotard top of her swimsuit framing her sunburnt shoulders. Poking at a computer tablet, she seemed to be coasting vaguely from one link or file to another, surfing videos—the squeaks of the computer speaker just audible around her.

I was drifting, as well, as I sat on the faded gray wood of the old, wobbly dock off to the side, dangling my feet down in the water while my daughter practiced her swimming back and forth across the green-gray lake. The younger children of other families splashed in the bright sun, with the sky in its frame of cliffs—too blue, really: almost false, and decorated with the kind of wispy clouds that only the hokiest artists would dare put in their paintings. And the long dusty-red striations of the canyon, capped with green-black pines. When I squint a little, those horizon-topping rows of trees have always looked to me like ancient caravans: camels and horses and people walking, heading off to trade

with the nearby mountains. And when I start float-
ing and stare up at them, I always get to thinking
that maybe I should have gone with them on their
journey. That maybe I should have done things differently. That maybe I have wasted my life.

Then the man on the inner tube awoke with a
shout as the rocks brushed against him—sitting up
suddenly, too hard and too fast, so the inner tube
squirted out to flip up in the air behind him and
dump him with a splash into the shallow water. I
think it must have been painful—those broken
stones down at the end of the lake *hurt*—and he
yowled, scrambling along on hands and knees after
the inner tube, trying to stand up and stumbling
each time as the rocks sliced at his tender feet, before he finally caught up with the spinning tube and
surged across it, belly first, puffing like a walrus.

My daughter pulled up, bobbing in the water
to see what the fuss was. The splashing children
all froze in the shallows. The woman in the hat
bounced to her feet, shielding her eyes with her

computer tablet while she stared anxiously down the lake till the startled man began paddling his slow way back up from the dam—at which point, interestingly, she turned to check on the children before the uneasy look faded from her face.

The lake is chillier than you'd expect on an early summer day; fed by a stream tumbling down from the hills, it's maybe twenty or thirty feet deep out in the middle, and never really warms up. Faith was trembling as she climbed up out of the water, so I wrapped her in a towel and hurried her to the car. The dust of the dirt road swirled up behind us as we drove back to town, a beige so light it looked in the rearview mirror like a white fog trailing after the car, while my shivering daughter leaned forward, almost touching the heater vents on the dashboard.

This broken western country is home for me; mountain lakes in the canyons hold echoes, and the presence of the past is what makes a moment rich with meaning, thick with memory. But the future: That's what makes the present important. That's what lends each moment significance and weight. That's what forces consequence into the choices we make and the paths we choose.

We cannot drift, really. We cannot coast forever. We cannot agree with a shrug to leave our children a world of murder and war and corruption and hurt souls. Though there is no final victory that we can achieve on our own, still we must work so that things don't worsen. To have children is to look to the future and glimpse the consequence of the present moment. To have children is to understand what it means that down at the end of the easy stream, the rocks are sharp and the water cold.

III

BAH. DESCRIBING THOSE opposing eastern and western landscapes, I make it sound as though no place were right, when, in fact, we had wonderful times everywhere we lived. Wonderful friends,

wonderful cityscapes, and wonderful country re-
treats. Wonderful Christmases, for that matter,
with parties and presents, street musicians playing the season's carols, and offerings of eggnog and
mulled wine. Beautiful trees, with perfect propor-
tions, and those handblown glass ornaments from
Egypt to hang on them. The big Franciscan parish
we attended in Washington, and the little tucked-
away church in New York, where we'd go to hear
the Christmas Mass in Latin.

Food, as well—and food, and yet more food.
There was our traditional Christmas Eve dinner
of ham, baked brie, and *fruktsuppe,* the Scandinavian dried-fruit soup the Lutheran settlers out on
the prairie would make in remembrance of their
homeland. (They would also celebrate the holiday
with *lutefisk,* dried Norwegian codfish rehydrated
with lye and boiled to the consistency of soggy
newspaper, but there were limits on how much tradition Lorena and I were willing to stomach.) And
we had goose and apple stuffing, and wild rice and

salt-wilted salads, and oven-fried potatoes, and cranberries. Always cranberries. An impossibly rich form of *bûche de Noël,* as well: that Parisian Christmas dessert rolled to look like a tree branch, using the recipe my older sister brought back from France. She loved all things French in those days, and so, naturally, we teased her by calling it "Frog Log," which, somewhere along the way, simply became the ongoing family name for the thing. Lorena would head out to the stores each December, in search of green gummy candies shaped like frogs—the decoration my daughter still insists is a necessary element of the dessert. I live in terror of any of our French friends finding out.

Every year Lorena would dragoon Faith and me into helping with the glass jar canning of the apple butters and peach chutneys and watermelon pickles to send as Christmas presents to friends and family. As Christmas approached, she'd spend days making chocolate truffles. Hard meringue, too, shaped like mushrooms. (I'm still not sure why: what about mushrooms says *Christmas?*) And, one year, the taffy she made us pull, which burned our buttered fingers and stuck to the wax paper and wore out our arms and still never set up properly. A black fruitcake, too, heavy as uranium and almost as radioactive, made from Emily Dickinson's directions. An odd sort of Amherst recipe, written just like her poems: all short, quick lines and lots of dashes.

Christmas was our time for charity, as well, although some of that came to us from the New Testament via the U.S. tax code. Only in December, the end of the year, could we figure how much we could afford for the annual gift to the local school's scholarship fund, the church, the organizations we support. We'd take our turns sitting with the donation collection box at the shopping mall, and we'd drop off cans and dried goods at the food bank. The Salvation Army kettles, too: when Faith was very young, she would beg for coins, corner after corner, because she loved the way the bell-ringing Santas smiled when she dropped them in.

All of it was Christmas. Just Christmas, rolling down upon us like an avalanche, wherever we were. Still, there's a reason to think more deeply about the places in which we live, you and I—to understand our homes as they really are: locations in a spiritual geography. From the Church Fathers to John Paul II, Christianity has a long tradition of viewing the world this way. The desert, Balzac once wrote, holds everything because it holds nothing. The beauty of the bleak and empty, the holiness of the silent and the blank: if you cannot call up that mood in yourself, then half of human literature will seem insane to you, and half of human psychology will appear alien and bizarre. Yes, the cold mind of hermits can be frozen into immobility. Still, those isolated figures understand something real about the world, and their opposites, the overheated people whose minds are *never* cool—how can they see the whole of human experience, the shadows that define the lights?

But, then, we have in our lives the lush and the

full as well. The rich, the lively: a different landscape of splendor and shared abundance. God
warms his hands at human fires, at family hearths
and public flames, for this is how he made us. We
are political animals, and we live in packs. We are
social creatures, and we dwell with other people.
We are cultured beings, and we seek friendship by
our very nature. Yes, crowds can stifle and mobs can
kill the spirit. But if you cannot call up in yourself
the warmer mood of love for neighbors, of happi-
ness in throngs, then the other half of human literature and psychology will seem unreal. We have a
word to describe such people. We call them lonely.

The imaginations of the prophets, of the mystics
and the saints, are full of this kind of geographical
division: Should the Ark of the Covenant stay at
the country camp at Shiloh or be brought into the
city temple in Jerusalem? Is faith best found in the
anchorite's lonely cell or among fellow believers in
a crowded cathedral? The history of human experience knows such distinctions, and it maps them

onto the physical world. To call the result *symbolism* would be a mistake. The word *symbol* is just another expression of the modern thinning and demythologizing of reality. Those places were once something more than symbols. They were trumpet cries that echoed across the universe. They were weights that tugged on the imagination. They were magnetic poles that influenced our compass readings. They were the ley lines in the cartography of the soul.

We seem to walk such trackless land today. Our maps have faded, and we wander in circles, each of us a lost surveyor of the wilderness of life. When, in 1773, Samuel Johnson and his friend James Boswell visited the wrecked medieval monasteries on the island of Iona off the Scottish coast, they went *expecting*—as they both wrote to describe it— that the ruins would force them to contemplate the divine, the saintly, and the lingering influence of ancient prayer. Where shall we go for something like that now? Without a spiritual geography, the known world is terra incognita. A place without trails or pathbreakers' marks. A quest without meaning or goal.

Except—well, what about Christmas? There's something geographical deep down at the greeny heart of the holiday, underneath the overlays of clinging tinsel and flimsy ornaments. Of portly men pretending to be Santa Clauses and bristly plastic kits pretending to be trees. Cotton flocks that imitate snow, polystyrene leaves that counterfeit holly, those little battery-operated lights that mimic candles. All that plastic stuff, piled on top of Christmas.

Actually, I enjoy the sillier manifestations of the season. This year, one of our neighbors set up large inflatable figures in the Christmas snow, around the curve of the street that runs by the Episcopalians' little sandstone church in Hot Springs: Santa and a candy cane and the like. And every time we drive past, we wave at the goofy reindeer, who looks just like a giant version of one of Faith's old stuffed animals. And why not? It's part of the wonderful preposterousness of the season.

Still, I think I understand what leads some people to reject the shape that Christmas has these days. I have a friend in New York, for example, who has deliberately turned his back on all the commercialized falsity of Christmas. A deep believer—a young mystic who has chosen to live his life very simply—Mark goes out every December to find a small branch, a fallen leafless stick, for Christmas. He stands it up in a pot on his table, decorates it with a handmade ornament or two, and sets a paper star on top. One year he added a few pieces of popcorn strung on a thread, but I think he thought them a disruption, for they were absent the next Christmas when I stopped by to give him his annual gift of apple butter and Emily Dickinson fruitcake.

It's the hard center of the holiday, of course, that he wants not to be distracted from. He loves the discipline of Advent, because the run-up to

Christmas, in the church's calendar, focuses his thoughts and prayers on the great gift of that holy time: on God's descending in the flesh, on the Blessed Virgin's assent to the celestial purpose, and on the beginning and end of things, the Alpha and Omega that is Christ. He tries to ignore, as best he can, the overblown, overexcited cheapening of Christmas in the loud blare of the season, since it only makes him sad—or angry, or crazy, or depressed, or something; distracted, at any rate—to see that fundamental moment, when the divine appeared in human form, smothered under layers of phony "Happy Holidays!" cheer.

I envy, in many ways, the intentionally minimal, prayerful life that Mark lives. For that matter, I'm pretty sure he's a better man than I am, and that mood of his—the distaste for the snake oil of commercialized Christmas—is something I can call up in myself, if I set my mind to it. Still, as the years have gone by, I've come to think that Mark is wrong. I've grown to believe that he's missing some of the ways in which God can turn anything to his purpose. Some of the ways, for that matter, in which human beings respond to the rich, abundant experience of God. When we see the busy sidewalks—when we're buffeted by the shoppers hurrying past the tricked-up Christmas decorations on the storefronts—we shouldn't imagine we're watching people who are smothering the impulse of religion. These are ordinary folk, trying to celebrate the season. They sometimes falter, as we all do, and they're often confused, as we all are. But they grasp in some profound manner that a *real* thing comes toward us in December, and they layer it over with whatever fake or genuine finery they can find—not to hide it but to honor it.

Think of it this way: As we wander our modern wilderness, our unmapped territory, Christmas is a compass. It always follows the guiding light of the star over Bethlehem, and the line of that Christmas compass—like a surveyor's transit or theodolite—can orient us in the spiritual geography of our lives.

No place in which I've lived has seemed complete, all by itself. And yet, at play in the summer lands, at work in the fall and winter cities, hoping for the spring: through it all, Christmas has remained true and unswerving. The rush of days, the piles of presents, the trees and the food and the ornaments and the carols and the tinsel and the plastic bunches of fake mistletoe and all the rest—these are not distractions but *testimonies* to the thing. If you step back, just a little, you can see them for what they are. They join, in the mad dance of the season, to make a pattern. They orient themselves to the giant compass needle that could lead us to the truth.

You want to feel the spirit of Christmas, the magnetic pull of the holiday? Be the shepherds. Keeping watch over their flocks by night, there in the Gospel of Luke, they suddenly saw a great light that illuminated the darkness all around them and heard the angel saying, "Fear not." And they simply believed, gathering themselves and walking down the hill to find the manger "and see this thing which is come to pass, which the Lord hath made known unto us." It's the innocence and trust, the simplicity, of the shepherds that ought to speak to us, guide us, teach us how to live in the season. These were country folk, and their simple faith is the first pattern of Christmas.

And while you're being the shepherds, be the Wise Men, too—for their faith is the other pattern of Christmas, the second way to live and enact the season. These were city dwellers and learned people, as they appear in the Gospel of Matthew, and when a great star appeared in the sky, they followed their intellectual curiosity and—why not?—journeyed off to discover where it led. They brought gifts, because they wanted to honor the newborn king for whom they were searching, and they imagined they might actually find him. They had the wisdom, in other words, to use their sophistication and intelligence to examine honestly the clues the world offered them and to seek the truth for its own sake, whatever it might prove to be.

IV

I SAW THE shepherds and Wise Men once, I think.
I had been by myself most of a winter drive, the cold
wind whistling through the door and dashboard
leaks in the pickup my father had given me. I'd been
alone up the red-rock canyon, past the trout hatch-
ery, rimmed with ice, and the gemstone-and-fossil
shop, shuttered for the winter. Alone past the Trappist monastery's roadside stand, where the novices
and young monks sell their cheese and honey, fresh
bread if you come by early enough, at a long pine
table through the summer months, abandoned
and dusted with snow that December. Alone over
the pass and down into the winter meadow below.
Alone across the valley floor of yellow-brown buffalo grass and up into the tree line on the other side.

But as the truck strained, shifting down into
second gear to climb the winding road back into
the hills, I began to imagine others rode with me,

sitting beside me on that pickup's long bench seat. Talking and arguing, making distinctions, explaining their views, attempting to teach me. I was probably a little crazed by that point. I'd been up for two days, after an exhausting week of travel, and I was trying just to get home for Christmas before I collapsed or had an accident. And somewhere in my sleep-deprived mind, the ghosts came to visit.

Or lecture or contend or clarify or instruct. There was that Irishman, a literature teacher I'd once had, who told me again the story about his thirtieth birthday, when he'd drunkenly flushed his grandfather's watch down the toilet, shouting to his friends and neighbors, "Time doesn't matter anymore."

And Rosemary, a neighbor from my parents' days in Salt Lake City, with a slow, calm kind of motherly wisdom. The professor from over on First Avenue, too: another Salt Lake acquaintance, who had written a book about urban legends and told me all-American fantasy tales about vanishing hitch-hikers and hook-handed criminals: *You can always tell it's modern folklore,* he explained, *if the story starts with something like "This really happened to a friend of my cousin's . . ."* A quietly insane magazine writer I used to visit, who insisted that the poet Wallace Stevens really had become a Catholic on his Hartford deathbed, whatever his daughter now says. *Connecticut's conversions stun.* My second-grade teacher from South Dakota, Mrs. Winton, who'd given me for Christmas a book about a young Sioux boy on a quest to find a rare white buffalo, and who returned to help me, as she had before, through the puzzle I was finding life.

I sat for a while in companionable silence with a ranch hand I had known, as he worked neat's-foot oil into a stiff piece of bridle leather and gestured from time to time toward the passing hills, as though to remind me of God's good creation. I tried to answer Avery's sharp questions about my confused views of theology and the order of this world.

A swirling, constantly shifting cloud of witness: Francis, spouting lines of German poetry I didn't understand, and Richard expounding the Last Supper, and Mary logically ticking off the points of an argument about American schooling, and my aunt patiently teaching me how to wash the dishes when I was young.

The small-town pilot I'd talked with for hours, fogged in at the Detroit airport, who was heading back to Ohio to dust crops in his bi-wing plane. Sally, Uncle Joe, an old construction foreman, that farmer in Alliance, Nebraska, who was so smart about western water and the spring's snowmelt: Some of them were dead, long slipped away. Others I hadn't seen for years. But they came, anyway, to visit me on the drive home through the Christmas hills. All that wisdom, all that knowledge, pleading, pointing, shouting at me to see this world as it really is. To open my eyes and just *see*.

Actually see, as it happens—for I caught, at an angle through the trees, a glimpse of a dog darting across the road ahead, and slowed just in time to keep from plowing into a flurry of thick-wooled sheep as I came around the bend. Sheep are odd-looking animals in the winter. Odd-looking animals at any time, as far as that goes, and maybe especially in the spring, after the shearing, when they resemble nothing so much as confused recruits, unable to explain how they ended up standing naked in a new-green field. Still, in the winter, they wear a peculiar puffy look, as though they had pulled on multiple sweaters, one over another, and topped it off with one of those Scandinavian knit hats that flop around their ears and droop over their foreheads.

It was there, by the little wooden chapel in the hills, that the sheep stopped me, spilling across the road. I had driven past the building maybe a dozen times over the years, a tiny place painted in those old Forest Service colors of washed-out brown with yellow trim, and I've never known who used it for services or why. Never seen the chapel open or alive, for that matter, and if I'd thought about it, I would have assumed it was boarded up and shuttered for the winter.

Still, the lamps were on in the shed-sized church late that December afternoon, in the failing sun of the days before Christmas, and the light appeared to be shining not *out,* somehow, but *in.* I know, of course, when I stop to think about it, that the light had to be coming from inside the church, but that wasn't how it seemed at the time. To my tired, burning eyes, the yellow beams looked as though they ran in the opposite direction: like a beacon, an arrow of light, over the milling sheep, across the little yard, and in through the windows to illuminate, in sharp detail, the interior scene.

I can close my eyes and see it again, in all its precision: The blizzard of white-sweatered, odd-faced sheep, roiling like a confused avalanche across the pavement. A long-haired black dog, streaks of brown and gray in his fur, nipping at the sheep to move, finally move, down the road toward the gate into a nearby field. The herders with their crocks—

two of them, wearing thick gloves and stained parkas, whistling directions to the dog. And the people in the chapel, a young woman and a middle-aged man dressed in holiday clothes, red and green, putting up Christmas decorations.

Simple things: a plaster crèche, maybe half life-size, with kneeling shepherds and Wise Men bearing gifts, and Joseph and Mary, and an empty manger where the Christ child would lie. Some pine branches from the woods in the man's arms. A pair of poinsettias, out on the doorstep. A red piece of cloth draped on the wooden pulpit. All of it illuminated by the arrow of light, like the path of a star, that swept across the hills and into that chapel. Then the snowy drifts of sheep were past, the people in the chapel moved out of sight, and I started up again through the canyons, driving home for Christmas.

But in my sleepy, half-crazed way, I had seen it, for a moment—the truth, the universe as it really is, the geography of our souls. You see it, too, don't you? Christmas isn't a day or even a season. It isn't a symbol for our better feelings or the sentimental sum of our memories. It isn't a celebration, and it isn't an anniversary. Oh, in a certain sense, it's all those things, but it's always *more,* if only we open our eyes and see. Just see. Christmas is the compass needle that points us toward God. The star shining for the Wise Men. The angels singing for the shepherds. Christmas is the illuminated path across the wilderness of life, our map to this world, and if we follow it—if we surrender, joyfully, to it— Christmas will lead us where we need to go.

Acknowledgments

I'M SUCH A slow writer that, to finish even this small book, I had to raid sentences, paragraphs, and whole sections of work I've published over the years in the *Wall Street Journal,* the *Weekly Standard,* Amazon's Kindle Singles ebook series, the annual book anthologies of *Best Spiritual Writing of the Year* and *Best Christian Writing of the Year,* and elsewhere. Few thanks comes to editors at such publications: if everything goes well, they receive no notice; if something goes wrong, they get the blame. So let me, for once, pour out my gratitude for the editors I've been lucky enough to work with—especially Claudia Anderson and Richard Starr, David Blum, Erich Eichman, and John Wilson.

The idea for a new collection of Christmas essays came from my agent, Cathy Hemming, who will forgive me, I hope, for the fact that it got a little transmogrified along the way. My editor at Crown/Random House, Gary Jansen, improved the text enormously, and I owe a debt to Brian Murray, Sally Thomas, and other friends who looked over various drafts and gave me more help than I deserved.

Of course, that's the way of much in life, isn't it—that we receive such unearned and unexpected gifts? It's what happens most Christmases, with the presents under the tree. It's what happened that first Christmas, two thousand years ago, when God descended in the flesh and gave us more, so much more, than we deserve.